# HOUSE

*of*

# WAR

# HOUSE

## *of*

# WAR

## ISLAM'S JIHAD AGAINST THE WORLD

## G.M. DAVIS, PH.D.

 WND Books

# HOUSE OF WAR

Published by WND Books, Washington, D.C. WND Books is a registered trademark of WorldNetDaily.com, Inc. ("WND")

Book designed by Mark Karis

WND Books are distributed to the trade by:
Midpoint Trade Books
27 West 20th Street, Suite 1102
New York, New York 10011
WND Books are available at special discounts for bulk purchases. WND Books also publishes books in electronic formats. For more information call (541) 474-1776 or visit www.wndbooks.com.

Paperback ISBN: 978-1-938067-98-3
eBook ISBN: 9780979267178

Library of Congress Cataloging-in-Publication Data

Davis, G. M.
House of war : Islam's jihad against the world / G. M. Davis, producer of the documentary film Islam: What the West Needs to Know.
    pages cm
Includes bibliographical references and index.
    ISBN 978-1-938067-98-3 (pbk.)
    1. Islam--Controversial literature. 2. Jihad.  I. Title.
    BP169.D38 2015
    297.2'72--dc23
                              2015011971

Printed in the United States of America
15 16 17 18 19 EBM 9 8 7 6 5 4 3 2 1

For Z. with love.

And in memory of the countless victims of the religion of Muhammad, through the centuries and today.

# CONTENTS

# PREFACE TO THE PAPERBACK EDITION

FROM BAD TO WORSE APTLY SUMS up the course of events since the publication of the first edition of this book in 2006. Islamic violence continues to flare around the globe, in Islamic countries but also in the West where, a few weeks before these words were written, twelve French journalists and others were massacred in their Parisian offices by Muslim jihadists out to "right a wrong" when *Charlie Hebdo* satirized their Prophet. The murderers were, it is now plain, acting self-consciously on religious motives, perhaps recalling the killing of Kab bin Al-Ashraf, a poet in Medina who had ridiculed Muhammad while he preached there, or one of several others during the life of the Prophet whom he had killed for insulting Islam (see chapter 4). The gunmen, eventually hunted down and slain by French police, died as martyrs according to the dictates of their god, who promises paradise to those who "fight in his cause and kill and are killed, a promise binding on him in truth" (Koran 9:111).

Overseas in the Islamic world, the West, led by the United States, insists on pulling every cork from every bottle and releasing the genie of jihad that the quasi-secular dictatorships of Saddam Hussein, Mubarak, Ghaddafi, and Assad once kept a lid on. Boldly flying in the face of all possible reason and evidence, the United States has unleashed her stupendous military machine to bring the blessings of "democracy" to lands and peoples wholly unsuited for it. Predictably, the result has not been genuine democratization in those countries but rather Islamization with its concomitant suppression of civil liberties, persecution of religious minorities, economic chaos, and nurturing of jihadist terrorism. The bad quasi-secular dictatorships of the Middle East have been replaced with far worse Islamic "democracies," which swing from tyranny to anarchy and back again, providing fertile ground for jihadist groups whose violent aspirations are in no way limited to their own societies. It is worth pointing out the consequences of American backing of Islamic movements in the past: it was the American-backed mujahideen in Afghanistan in the 1980s and Bosnia in the 1990s that would go on to establish the international terrorist infrastructure that made 9/11 possible (see John Schindler's *Unholy Terror*).

But the problem is much more than just terrorism. This author, and a handful of others in the English language, have been trying to awaken the public and its leaders to the very unpleasant reality that Islam, one of the worlds great religions and boasting more than a billion adherents, comprises a fundamentally violent political ideology that poses an existential threat to Western societies. This is the sort of news that gets messengers shot, and that is what has happened figuratively— sometimes literally—to those who have tried to introduce the reality of the Islamic danger into mainstream discourse. Today's coiffured, airhead newsreaders are delighted to tell us with this-just-in gravitas about the latest "Islamist" terrorist atrocity but will not permit (or will not be permitted by the producer dictating in their ear) analysis of the origins of the ideology that would induce someone to so ruthlessly murder his fellow human beings. This author himself enjoyed fifteen seconds of fame when he declaimed on a major television news network that the origins of Islamic violence are to be found in the Koran and the life of Muhammad—a statement that got his satellite feed cut while a roundtable of critics heaped scorn on his prejudicial ignorance.

It seems a permanent fixture of this world of ours that an optimistic lie is accepted far more readily than a sober truth. Nonetheless, we persist. Big things have small beginnings, and bringing Western Civilization about to face the Islamic danger will not be the work of one or a few. Indeed, it may not happen at all, but for those with the opportunity, great or small, to take a stand, it must be attempted.

# PREFACE

IN ALL QUOTATIONS IN THIS BOOK, my additions are given in braces, { }. All other parenthetical punctuation—( ), [ ], < >, etc.—are those of the original source or translator. I use the standard modern English spelling of "Koran" but include other renderings ("Kuran," "Quran," etc.) when those spellings appear in other sources. I have kept intact the somewhat awkward language and punctuation used by the translators of the Islamic texts lest I inadvertently alter their meaning. I have omitted accent marks in all translations from the Arabic because I find them cumbersome. References to the Koran, both my own and those of quoted sources, are given as the *sura* (chapter) followed by the verse (e.g., Sura 9:29).

This is not a work of original scholarship nor is it meant to be a general education on Islam. It is intended rather to provide an antidote to the uncritical acceptance of Islam as a religion that means no harm to our civil, social, and personal arrangements. The arguments and evidence advanced in this book rely heavily on authors who have been plowing this ground for years (including Andrew Bostom, Paul Fergosi, Ibn Warraq, Robert Spencer, Serge Trifkovic, and Bat Ye'or), and I encourage the reader to consult their works.

I acknowledge here a few people who helped in the preparation of the original hardcover edition of this book. Robert Spencer was very kind in answering a number of factual questions. He as well as Serge Trifkovic, Gary Bauer, and the venerable Bill Buckley (RIP) were also kind enough to give the manuscript a look and provide their thoughts. Most of all, I need to thank Bryan Daly, my collaborator on the documentary, *Islam: What the West Needs to Know*, which was the primary inspiration for this book. Regarding the paperback edition, thanks to WorldNetDaily for their willingness to take on the project, and thanks especially to my wife for providing encouragement and valuable feedback. Others who wish to be anonymous shall remain so. They know who they are.

By means of shrewd lies, unremittingly repeated, it is possible to make people believe that heaven is hell—and hell heaven. The greater the lie, the more readily it will be believed.

—ADOLF HITLER

# INTRODUCTION

THE SPECTACULAR ATTACKS OF SEPTEMBER 2001 on the United States and numerous sucessive atrocities around the world have brought Islam forcefully to the Western consciousness. But far from concluding that violence done in the name of Islam suggests that Islam itself is violent, Western leaders have, with remarkable consistentcy, gone out of their way to affirm that Islam is a peaceful religion that in no way condones the violence done in its name. To wit:

"No religion condones the murder of innocent men, women, and children. But our actions were aimed at fanatics and killers who wrap murder in the cloak of righteousness; and in so doing, profane the great religion in whose name they claim to act."
—BILL CLINTON, US PRESIDENT, AUGUST 20, 1998

"We honor the universal values that are embodied in Islam—love of family and community, mutual respect, the power of education, and the deepest yearning of all: to live in peace. Values that can bring people of every faith and culture together, strengthen us as people, and, I would argue, strengthen the United States as a nation."
—HILLARY CLINTON, US FIRST LADY, JANUARY 21, 1999

"We are all human beings, and we all believe that we should do unto others as we would have done unto us. And I think the message is clear, as we heard this morning: Islam is a religion for peace."
—KOFI ANNAN, UN SECRETARY-GENERAL, SEPTEMBER 14, 2001

"The doctrine and teachings of Islam are those of peace and harmony. I read the Koran—the god of the Koran is merciful and forgiving. It is a whole teaching dedicated to building peace in the world. . . "
—TONY BLAIR, BRITISH PRIME MINISTER, SEPTEMBER 19, 2001

"While these killers choose their victims indiscriminately, their attacks flow from an ideology and a terrifying vision for the world. Their acts are evil, but they're not insane. Some call this evil Islamic radicalism; others, militant jihadism; still others, Islamo-fascism. Whatever we choose to call this enemy, we must recognize that this ideology is very different from the tenets of the great religion of Islam."
—GEORGE W. BUSH, US PRESIDENT, NOVEMBER 14, 2005

"No religion is responsible for violence and terrorism. People are responsible for violence and terrorism.... They are not religious leaders, they are terrorists. And we are not at war with Islam, we are at war with people who have perverted Islam."
—BARACK OBAMA, US PRESIDENT, FEBRUARY, 18, 2015

In light of such uniformity of opinion across so many different parties and persuasions, one is tempted to suspect collusion. However, absent evidence to the contrary, it is unwarranted to assume that so many Western leaders are being systematically disingenuous. Indeed, even if they do harbor divergent private sentiments about Islam, public policy cannot help but conform to public positions so persistently affirmed. But if we are to defend ourselves against an enemy who claims Islam as his guiding principle, it is imperative that we come to understand Islam itself. In particular, we must ask the question: Are our representatives correct that Islam is a religion of peace, something that can coexist with our own civilization? Or does Islam contain within itself the cause of the violence and terrorism done in its name?

It is the contention of this book that the idea that Islam is a religion of peace is fundamentally, totally, and disastrously wrong. In fact, *Islam is intrinsically violent; it is the impetus for modern terrorism, and its doctrines necessitate that the only possible relationship between Islamic civilization and non-Islamic civilization is war or subjugation.*

Engaging in violence against non-Muslims is not a fringe idea but a central tenet of Islam. Unlike traditional forms of Christianity, Islam is less a personal faith than a political ideology that exists in a permanent state of war with the rest of the world. The Islamic holy texts, while they address the spiritual life of the individual, also outline a social, governmental, and economic system that is divinely enjoined to pursue dominion over the entire earth. *Islam* means "submission" or "surrender" and a *muslim* is "one who submits." Societies and individuals who do not submit to Islamic rule exist in a state of rebellion against *Allah* (God) and must be forcibly brought into submission. The spectacular acts of Islamic terrorism in the late twentieth and early twenty-first centuries are only recent manifestations of a global war that Islam has been waging for nearly fourteen centuries.

Notwithstanding cries of racism, intolerance, hatemongering,

Islamophobia, etc., it is imperative to address the issue of Islamic violence squarely and candidly in a time of national and global danger. Over the course of its fourteen-hundred-year history, Islam has demonstrated that violence is essential to its makeup; violence is not a peripheral characteristic that arises only in times of crisis but an integral component that finds expression in a variety of historical circumstances. This is the simple, glaring truth that stares the world in the face today—and has stared it in the face at other times in history—but which few seem willing to contemplate. Yet, however difficult to accept, the fact is that we are in a global religious conflict with an adversary who intends to destroy or conquer us and who has been hard at work at both for fourteen centuries.

# PART I

# THE PROBLEM

# 1

# OBSCURING THE ISSUE

LIKE OTHER RELIGIONS, ISLAM GENERALLY SEES the universe in terms of good and evil, but unlike a religion such as Christianity, in Islam good and evil have expressly political significance. The notion in the Western world that religion is a mostly private matter centered on the faith of the individual is a concept alien to Islam. It is the *Umma,* the global Islamic community, that is the focus and end of Islamic thought and practice rather than the individual believer. While in some ways the Umma may be analogized to a Christian church, the former knows no separation between it and the realm of terrestrial politics. The Umma is less a church than it is a global nation that transcends conventional political boundaries. Good and evil then necessarily translate to the political realm in which two spheres battle one another in perpetual conflict: the House of Islam and the House of War. The House of Islam (*dar al-Islam*) comprises territory where Islamic law (*Sharia*) is the law of the land, while the House of War (*dar al-harb*) comprises lands not ruled by Sharia. The House of Islam is enjoined by Allah to fight the House of War until the latter is permanently assimilated into the former and Sharia holds sway unimpaired. The term *jihad,* which literally means "struggle," denotes the effort, military and otherwise, to bring new lands into the House of Islam. While the state of war between the Islamic and non-Islamic worlds is sometimes hot and sometimes cold, it is permanent until such time that Sharia law reigns supreme.

It is critical to understand that Islam's division of the world into the House of Islam and the House of War is not merely a question of practice but is one of principle. In the Islamic worldview, Sharia law (which comprises the commandments of the Koran and the precedents and teachings of Muhammad) is the only legitimate basis of government; any social or political system not based on Sharia violates the edicts of Allah himself and constitutes not merely a political transgression but a form of sacrilege. While every religion distinguishes between believers and unbelievers, Islam draws a capital distinction between political-legal regimes: those in submission (Islam) to Allah's law and those in rebellion. It is the political-strategic contest between the two that is of the utmost importance in the Islamic worldview.

Because most Westerners fail to grasp the political nature of Islam, they speak about Islamic violence and terrorism as if they bear no relationship to Islam proper. They imagine that acts of terrorism can only be irrational and pathological and something that all sensible people—Muslim and non-Muslim—must deplore. But the notion that authentic religion in general is somehow naturally peaceful is a Western prejudice rather than a demonstrated truth. In order to understand the origins of Islamic violence we must be willing to discard many comforting assumptions and try to see the world from an Islamic point of view. Acquiring a basic grasp of the Islamic worldview does not require learning Arabic or taking a pilgrimage to Mecca. But it does require the investment of some time and thought to become familiar with the origins and history of Islam and the life of its founder, Muhammad, whose teachings and examples lie at the core or Islamic belief and practice. Few Westerners have made such an investment, preferring instead to assume blindly that Muslims practicing their faith are not so very different from the followers of other religions. That assumption is not merely wrong, it is deadly.

Of course, Muslims (like Christians, Jews, and members of any religion) often fail to understand or live up to the standards of their faith. But what distinguishes Islam from other religions is that when it is correctly understood and practiced, it actively seeks the subjugation or destruction of everything that is not itself. Non-Islamic religions may seek the conversion or evangelization of others, and their devotees may even employ force against others from time to time, but Islam is the only religion whose basic animating principles pit it against the rest of the world in a struggle to the death, ensuring that war is the natural and obligatory state of affairs.

The dichotomy between the House of Islam and the House of War is suggestive of other, more modern ideologies such as Communism and National Socialism. Both Communism and National Socialism divide the world into two permanently warring spheres. While Communism and National Socialism find inspiration in economic or racial theories of history, Islam is inspired by Allah and Muhammad even while it shares the expansionary political goals of the other two. Islam is not only a religion that orients the individual and collective towards a conception of divinity but is also a political system divinely ordained to encompass the entire earth. Islam is in fact a kind of state, a polity that transcends conventional political boundaries.

Once one appreciates that Islam is as much political-territorial as it is religious, one can see that for an individual or society to refuse the rule of Islam is not so much an act not of impiety but of rebellion, which is properly dealt with by force. It is also easy to understand the obligation of Muslims to kill apostates (Muslims who leave Islam) since defecting from Islam constitutes not an act of conscience but of treason.

The secular West would do well to bear in mind that, however strange it may seem today, for most of history civilizations and peoples were defined by the gods they worshipped, and it was the character of those gods that shaped individual and collective action. It has only been in the past few hundred years that the god one worships was eclipsed by apparently more important factors such as ethnicity, nationality, class, or political party. With the current resurgence of Islamic violence and cultural imperialism, we are cast back into the pre-modern paradigm. Today's preachers of multiculturalism and tolerance who champion Islam at the expense of Western mores demonstrate ignorance of a suicidal order. They fail to recognize that true Islam embodies a multiculturalist's worst fears: an unwavering conviction in its own cultural superiority, a readiness to use force to spread its dominion, and a systematic disregard for those weaker than or different from itself.

It is also imperative for the West to discard the assumption (hubris, really) that its own principles and mores are universal. In particular, the sense of morality and justice derived from concepts of natural law that Christendom integrated into its tradition is almost entirely absent in Islam. All of the points of reference on the Islamic moral compass were established in the lifetime of the Prophet Muhammad. Only by appreciating

Muhammad and the environment in which his religion developed—the bloody anarchy of seventh century Arabia—can we adequately interpret the myriad acts of violence done in his name through history and today. The Prophet Muhammad enshrined the violent ways of seventh century Arabia in a religion with global ambitions. Islam has thus served as the vehicle by which the bloody practices of the Arabian tribal system have been thrust upon the globe. Islam legitimized the violence prevalent in Muhammad's day and made it a permanent aspect of Islam's social expression.

A favorite tactic of Islamic apologists when confronted with Islam's violent nature is to change the subject; the one thing they never seem to want to talk about is Islam itself. Defenders of Islam (Muslim and non-Muslim) are quick to point out that members of other faiths have been violent at times, but they will rarely discuss the details of Islam's origins, doctrines, or history. While it is true that Christians have acted violently at times, we may well ask: If Christians have fought and killed in the name of a God who explicitly commands love, humility, and turning the other cheek, what can we expect from followers of a religion that instructs them, in the words of the Koran, to "kill the unbelievers wherever you find them" (Sura 9:5)? While violence committed by Christians in the name of Christianity demonstrably violates their religion's tenets, violence committed by Muslims in the name of Islam explicitly fulfills theirs.

Westerners must also abandon the assumption that we can speak about concepts like justice and morality as if those words mean the same thing in Western and Islamic cultures. Islamic notions of justice are less akin to Christian notions than to pagan ones in which right and wrong are determined primarily by power. One might say that, whereas in Christianity God is powerful because he is good, in Islam Allah is good because he is powerful. While both Christians and Muslims speak of mercy and justice, their traditions interpret those concepts in very different ways. Islamic justice means the military and political supremacy of Muslims over non-Muslims in accord with Allah's will. The late Islamic religious leader Ayatollah Khomeini, who led a popular revolution in 1979 in one of the most populous Muslim countries, Iran, sums it up rather well:

> Islam makes it incumbent on all adult males, provided they are not disabled or incapacitated, to prepare themselves for the conquest of countries so that the writ of Islam {Sharia} is obeyed in every country in the world. . . . But those who study Islamic Holy War will understand why Islam wants to conquer the world. All the countries conquered by Islam or to be conquered in the future will be marked for everlasting salvation. For they shall live under Light Celestial {Sharia} Law.
>
> Those who know nothing of Islam pretend that Islam counsels against war. Those are witless. Islam says: Kill all the unbelievers just as they would kill you all! Does this mean that Muslims should sit back until they are devoured by [the unbelievers]? Islam says: Kill them, put them to the sword and scatter [their armies]. Does this mean sitting back until [non-Muslims] overcome us? Islam says: Kill in the service of Allah those who may want to kill you! Does this mean that we should surrender? Islam says: Whatever good there is exists thanks to the sword and in the shadow of the sword! People cannot be made obedient except with the sword! The sword is the key to Paradise, which can be opened only for the Holy Warriors!

There are hundreds of other psalms and hadiths {accounts of the Prophet Muhammad} urging Muslims to value war and to fight. Does all this mean that Islam is a religion that prevents men from waging war? I spit upon those foolish souls who make such a claim.[1]

Khomeini spits upon them; wishful-thinking Westerners embrace them. Islamic apologists invariably label Muslim leaders such as Khomeini as extremists, radicals, or Islamists (whatever on earth that is), but it is easy to see that their logic is circular. By the reasoning of the apologists, any Muslim who advocates violence is extreme, while any Muslim who does not is moderate. Thus, no matter how convincing the argument that Islam demands violence, they reflexively exclude such arguments as extreme. Nowhere are they willing to consider which interpretation is actually more correct in light of the Islamic sources themselves. Indeed, by their logic, today's Islamic apologists would wind up branding the Prophet Muhammad himself an extremist.

The unique problem with Muhammad is not that he fought wars and killed his enemies (as we will see)—many have done that. Nor is the problem that he claimed to be Allah's definitive prophet—many have done that as well. The problem is that through the combination of war and prophecy Muhammad forever established war and killing as acceptable (indeed, holy and noble) endeavors for all who would follow him. Bin Laden, Khomeini, or any other literate jihadist who takes the time to articulate his thinking is merely putting his money where his mouth is. The jihadists are those who take Islam seriously in word and deed. The entire Muslim world would be made up of what the apologists call radical Islamists if all Muslims took their faith as seriously as bin Laden or Khomeini. Violent behavior in the name of religion may be extreme from a Western point of view but not from an Islamic one.

The idea, however, that the world's fastest-growing religion, with well over a billion followers today, is seeking global hegemony and the destruction of other faiths, cultures, and civilizations is so appalling, so absolutely blasphemous to modern sensibilities, that it is simply not entertained by the intellectual establishment. Their thinking leads to the erroneous conclusion that because there would be no obvious solution to such a titanic problem there must not be a problem at all. Modern intellectuals lack the analytical and theoretical tools to make sense of such a thing. Politicians, academics, and pundits versed in the vocabulary of modern democracy are utterly unequipped to comprehend the nature and stakes of global religious warfare. It might have been typical for religions and civilizations to fight for supremacy in ages gone by—so their thinking runs—but certainly not in the age of democracy, human rights, and the United Nations.

When faced with the sort of violence witnessed throughout the past two decades around the world committed by Muslims in the name of their religion, it is tempting to see the perpetrators as mindless sadists possessed by an irrational bloodlust. Seeing them as blind fanatics allows us to avoid asking the uncomfortable question: What could motivate human beings to so single-mindedly seek the death of their fellows? But this is the question that must be asked if we are to come to understand this peculiar enemy. With deadly consistency, we have learned that the terrorists do not fit the profile of impoverished, scorned, illiterate thugs, but are often educated, pious, well-to-do men (and women) who seem to have plenty to live for in modern society. What would possess Osama bin Laden, a millionaire many times over, to live in a cave in Afghanistan and plot attacks certain to infuriate the most powerful nation on earth? The answer is an unshakable faith in his religion's promises that by doing so he will attain salvation and eternal bliss. This may sound crazy to the secular West, but to true Muslims it is a rational calculation arrived at through reflection and prayer.

Westerners will never be able to defend themselves against a motivated enemy if they see him as nothing more than a nut with a bomb. The jihadist's motivation is analogous (if far removed) to that of the countless Christian martyrs through history who suffered unimaginable hardship, torture, and death to gain salvation. Today's secular world, so far removed from its spiritual foundations, finds it nearly impossible to comprehend such a motivation. But those who regard Muslims as either barbarians or latent, freedom-loving Westerners—who see Islam as nothing more than an admixture of half-baked theological postulates that no one could possibly take literally—neglect the overwhelming evidence of history. Islam has demonstrated time and again a powerful capacity to motivate its faithful to organize in the name of Allah. Westerners may no longer be willing to sacrifice themselves for their gods, but they are impossibly naive if they think that the rest of the world shares their apathy.

Perhaps the greatest psychological barrier to accepting the reality that Islam is intrinsically violent is that the conflicts around the world between Muslims and non-Muslims then appear intractable. If, for instance, poverty or dictatorial government is the root cause of these conflicts, then the elimination of poverty or the institution of Western-style democracy would be the solution. If, however, the problem is a religious faith, the modern socio-political vocabulary has little to offer. Short of mass evangelization into a different religion (something sure to leave a sour taste in the mouth of modern intellectuals), the only option is to deprive the Muslim world of the physical means of inflicting violence on the non-Muslim world. But this is not a solution in the conventional sense, it is only damage control. It offers no plan for conclusively solving the problem. If violence is rooted in something as profound and inscrutable as religious belief, governed primarily by conscience and faith, then there is little chance of finding a definitive solution in this world.

But because a problem cannot be solved conclusively does not mean that there is no problem. While Western resources may not be capable of solving the problem of Islamic violence, the West's tremendous material and technological strength ought to be capable of containing it. But if the West persists in the false hope of solving the problem of Muslim violence once and for all (through democracy, capitalism, multiculturalism, sensitivity training, or whatever the next political vogue will be), it risks being unable to contain it and thus may bring down upon itself otherwise avoidable future disasters. The conclusions come to at the end of this book do not call for an anti-Islamic crusade but for awareness of what Islam is and a sober policy of containmentat at home and abroad.

The Islamic empires that covered three continents for thirteen centuries (roughly the late seventh through nineteenth centuries AD), far from the multicultural wonderland depicted in many recent popular books and documentaries, were places of institutionalized discrimination. Non-Muslim subjects were granted security of life and property only by acknowledging their inferiority and contributing to the economic health of the Muslim state. The genocidal wars of conquest that brought new lands into the House of Islam—the major waves of jihad—ended only when the infidel survivors were granted the *dhimma* (treaty of protection), were driven from their native lands, or were wiped out.

The status of these conquered *dhimmi* peoples depended on the regular payment of protection money to the Muslim overlords in the form of the Koranic poll tax (*jizya*) and other exactions. If the dhimmi was unable to pay, he forfeited protection and the jihad resumed. The much-cited great achievements of Islamic civilization were the products mainly of dhimmi peoples and of recent converts to Islam and were rarely the product of native believers from the Arabian homeland. From the time of Muhammad through the nineteenth century, the Islamic lands were slave-based societies that functioned largely through the exploitation of their indigenous, non-Muslim populations. The most feared troops of the Ottoman Empire (the forerunner of modern Turkey) were products of the *devshirme* system whereby Christian boys (mainly from the Balkans) were enslaved, forcibly converted, and transformed into tormentors of their own people. Known as janissaries, these warrior slaves inflicted untold suffering on the native Christian societies of Islamic occupied lands.

As the dhimmi populations of the empire dwindled over time due to conversion to Islam, massacre, deportation, and the many disabilities imposed by Sharia law, Islamic civilization lost its cultural, economic, and administrative manpower. Muslim societies today tend to be backward by modern standards chiefly due to the absence of sufficient numbers of dhimmis who in ages past provided them with their main source of technical know-how, cultural literacy, and administrative competence. As those dhimmi populations declined, Islamic societies declined with them.

Since Napoleon Bonaparte invaded Muslim Egypt in 1798 (and was expelled only by the intervention of another Western power, the British), the Muslim world has increasingly found itself forcibly integrated into the Western-dominated society of nations, with rules and manners foreign to it. The Ottoman Empire of the nineteenth and early twentieth centuries, economically and technically inferior to its European peers, had to play ball with the European powers in order to stave off disintegration. Islam's thousand years of glory—when Muslim armies were the terror of the world and huge Muslim hosts threatened to topple the capitals of Europe and Asia—was over. It is critically important to bear in mind, however, that Islam's relative quiescence during the modern era was due to the superiority of its adversaries rather than to any change in Islamic doctrine. Jihad has been just as central to Islam in the modern era as during its first millennium. It is just that the rise of the West and other non-Islamic powers have forestalled the kind of military activity seen in Islam's early days.

With the collapse of the Ottoman Empire after WWI and the end of the Caliphate (Caliph was the title of the spiritual and temporal leader of the Islamic Empire), the Muslim world lost the pre-eminent symbol of its unity and power. The Muslim nations now had to fend for themselves and integrate as best they could into the global nation-state game, which was dominated by the Western powers.

When the enormity of Islam's reverse at the hands of the non-Islamic colonial powers did eventually come home to the

Muslims, they reacted to it with millennial alarm—it was the first in the cataclysmic chain of events leading to the End of Time—or with the fatalistic assumption that Allah was angry with the Muslims for their shortcomings. He was therefore punishing them in a manner that seemed fitting to Him. None the less, that Dar al harb, the "House of War," that is the hostile non-Islamic world, should ultimately prevail over Dar al-Islam, the "House of Islam," seemed to them contrary to the long-term course of history as he had set it out in the Koran. The Koran seemed to them a somewhat more substantial authority upon which to rely in the longer term than that of the alien "hand that holds dominion . . . " {i.e., the non-Islamic powers} They therefore simply bided their time. They may not have been entirely misguided in doing so.[2]

For Muslims to be so obviously dominated by non-Muslims is an especially galling state of affairs and is only explained by the moral/spiritual decline of the Umma. It makes no sense that a well-ordered Islamic civilization should not dominate its non-Islamic counterparts. Unlike Christianity, Islam has doctrinal difficulty handling political inferiority. Christians, in light of the example of their Founder, should not be surprised when they are marginalized, subjugated, or otherwise poorly treated. In worldly terms, Christ was a great loser: He was rejected by the religious and political establishment; He explicitly rejected political action; and He suffered and died ignominiously all the while instructing His followers that their reward would come not in this life but in the eternal life to come. Muhammad, on the other hand, was a brilliant political and military success and preached the superiority of Islam in *this* world. Following the example of Muhammad, Muslims are supposed to dominate other peoples until the one true faith reigns triumphant over the entire earth. Whereas Christ's Kingdom is not of this world, the House of Islam is to enjoy preeminence in both this world and the next. Whereas Christ brought salvation through His own sacrificial death, Muhammad preached salvation through killing the enemies of Allah.

If Islamic civilization is relegated to inferior status in the political sphere, it thus follows that Islamic civilization is not well ordered and needs to return to its basic principles. While there are ongoing attempts to orient Islamic societies today toward dar al-harb in a systematically peaceful way (Turkey, Indonesia, Jordan come to mind) such efforts are perennially hampered by "fundamentalists" who point out, quite rightly, that Allah has ordained otherwise. Any peaceable, outward-looking Islamic society will be forever open to attack from orthodox Muslims who will regard it as heretical. The rise of the "Islamic State" in the provinces of Iraq and Syria in 2014 is a perfect example. Here a well-organized band of Sunni Muslims has successfully accused the governments of those countries of collaboration with infidels and heresy and thereby gained an impressive following. For decades, numerous peace-minded statesmen in the Islamic world have suffered violent deaths at the hands of their co-religionists precisely because they sought to make peace with Islam's enemies.

One oft-repeated hope in the West is that, even if Islam contains violent elements, an Islamic reformation will in due course defang the religion. The hope is that Muslim reformers will transform Islam into something that can coexist with the rest of the world, much like the Protestant reformers transformed Western

Christianity into something less doctrinaire. This hope suffers from many fallacies, most significantly the presumption that the essence of the religion is benevolent and that its violent tendencies have their origins elsewhere. In fact, the wave of Islamic violence in the late twentieth and early twenty-first centuries may be seen as Islam's way of getting back to basics and reassuming the mantle of jihad in the vein of Muhammad and his followers. With the growing incidence of global Muslim violence, the reformation of Islam is in fact energetically taking place.

Just as the Protestant reformers sought to decouple Christianity from worldly institutions they believed had corrupted it, so today's jihadists seek to free themselves and their faith from the unholy compromises made with the House of War. The critical difference in the two cases lies in the violent nature of Islam, which demands that any reformation of Islam march inexorably along a path of increased violence and conquest. Just as Christian reformers through the ages have sought to reinvigorate their faith by imitating Christ (however fallibly), so Muslim reformers today seek to imitate Muhammad. The very divergent behaviors result from the very different examples and teachings of the founders of those two religions. But before delving into the origins of Islam, we must first clear away the politically correct language that has so infected contemporary discourse and which renders a frank accounting of Islam's true nature impossible.

# 2

# BAD LANGUAGE

THE CHIEF BARRIER TODAY TO A better public understanding of Islam is sloppy language. Imprecision in language permits public personalities to sound as though they have grasped the problem even while avoiding the crux of the matter. To start with, let us take as an example the phrase "war on terror." Upon scrutiny, a war on terror makes as much sense as a war on blitzkrieg, bullets, or strategic bombing. Terror is a method, not a goal. The war on terror, like the "wars" on poverty and drugs of the last decades, is a war against an imaginary enemy that replaces the flesh and blood of the true enemy with an abstraction. The phrase "war on terror" implies that it is perfectly acceptable if the enemy seeks to destroy us—and, indeed, succeeds in doing so—as long as he does not employ "terror" in the process. One can only imagine what the reaction would have been following Pearl Harbor had President Roosevelt requested a declaration of war against sneak attacks. Fighting a "war" against "terror" permits the powers that be to avoid facing the awkward reality that we are in a war with Islam or, more precisely, that Islam is at war with us.

Terrorism, it should be obvious, is a tactic or stratagem used to advance a goal; it is the goal of Islamic terrorism that we must come to understand and this requires an understanding of Islam itself. And to examine Islam is to come to understand that it knows no separation of the secular and the religious; that it is, in fact, a system of government ordained by Allah to hold sway over the entire earth. No two systems of government can occupy the same place, and it is this fact that puts Islam in perpetual combat with the rest of the world.

We are assaulted today with a deluge of information reporting apparently random acts of violence around the world vaguely tied to Islam. We hear of rebels, insurgents, ethnic cleansing, conflict, guerillas, and of course the routine acts of terrorism occasionally punctuated by a major massacre. Pundits weave op-ed pieces and toss around talk show sound bites trying to shed light on the "underlying factors" of this perplexing violence. Invariably, however, contemporary analysts utilize language drawn from neo-modern categories that utterly fails to penetrate to the motivation of the perpetrators. We hear much about poverty, disenfranchisement, frustration, etc., which supposedly lead to extremism and terror. By this logic, we would be at a complete loss to explain the astonishing peaceful-ness of huge numbers of the world's disenfranchised poor who consistently fail to express their frustration through terrorism. What is almost never pointed out is the fact that the common denominator to most of the ongoing conflicts in the world today is the religion of Muhammad and its simple, compelling mes-sage to its faithful that they are to bring the dominion of Allah to the earth by force. But to blame a (non-Christian) religion for causing violence transgresses the unwritten speech codes of today, so instead we get righteous indignation toward "terrorism" but not toward the thought-system that spawns it.

The Western establishment's dogged attempts to shield

Islam from criticism by employing politically correct language ignores the plain state of affairs in the world today. Of the major world conflicts of the last three decades, it would be easier to list those that did not involve Islam. In contrast, the wars in the Sudan, the Ivory Coast, Nigeria, Chechnya, Algeria, Bosnia, Kosovo, East Timor, the Spice Islands, the Philippines, Somalia, Iraq, Israel, Afghanistan, Mauritania, Kashmir, and Thailand all include a self-identified Muslim fighting force. And that list does not include the major acts of international terrorism, the overwhelming preponderance of which are committed by Muslims in the name of their religion. Of the forty foreign terrorist organizations named by the US State Department, six of them are Communist, six nationalist, one Jewish, and fully twenty-seven of them Islamic.[1] Where on earth do Muslims get such ideas? Well, to begin with, there is the Koran:

> Sura 9:5. Then when the Sacred Months (the 1st, 7th, 11th, and 12th months of the Islamic calendar) have passed, then kill the *Mushrikun* (the disbelievers in the Oneness of Allah, idolaters, polytheists, pagans, etc.) wherever you find them, and capture them and besiege them, and prepare for them each and every ambush. But if they repent and perform *As-Salat* (*Iqamat-as-Salat* {the Islamic ritual prayers}), and give Zakat {alms}, then leave their way free. Verily, Allah is Oft-Forgiving, Most Merciful.

It is only when we understand Islam's explicit commands to commit violence—the requirement of the Muslim world to wage war against the non-Muslim world and the encouragement of individual Muslims to commit personal deeds of violence—that the myriad instances of Muslim violence come into focus.

While the particular reasons that any Muslim individual or group embarks on a course of violence surely include political, economic, and psychological factors, there is nonetheless something at the bottom of it all: the Islamic religion itself. That so many of the conflicts around the world today have proved so intractable is thanks to their common denominator, Islam, and its god who instructs his followers to commit violence against others for the purpose of spreading his dominion.

To be clear: we are talking about Islam—not Islamic fundamentalism, extremism, fanaticism, Islamo-fascism, or even that over-used euphemism Islamism. We are talking about Islam proper, Islam in its orthodox form as it has been understood and practiced by devout Muslims from the time of Muhammad to the present. As Mervyn Hiskett has observed:

> But the truth is, Islamic "fundamentalism," as the world has understood it . . . adds little, if anything, to what has always been inherent in Islam since the Koran was revealed. The collapse of {Western European} imperialism and the rise of the liberal ethic have simply removed the barriers that once so salubriously contained it.[2]

Most discussions of Islamic terrorism—explained away as the result of fanaticism or some such thing—leave unanswered the question of why Islamic fanaticism takes the peculiar form that it does. A Buddhist fanatic might commit self-immolation or a Christian fanatic might sell his possessions and forsake the world, but neither would crash an airliner into a skyscraper or hijack an elementary school (as happened in Beslan, Russia in September 2004) with the intent of killing as many civilians as possible. Whatever the contributory influence of poverty, illiteracy, the legacy of Western colonialism, United States foreign policy, etc., at the heart of the terrorism problem is Islam itself. We will see in following chapters how the tactics of hostage taking and beheading practiced by Islamic terrorists today have explicit precedent in the Koran and the life of Muhammad. No matter how we may try to avoid it, an objective analysis of Islamic history, practices, and holy texts leads to the inescapable conclusion that violence against non-Muslims is essential to the Islamic faith. Violence has been integral to Islam ever since the Prophet Muhammad set the Arabian Peninsula ablaze in the seventh century, and it is fantasy to think that we will be able to undo that basic fact.

The mounting episodes of Islamic terrorism in the late twentieth and early twenty-first centuries are due largely to the geo-strategic changes following the end of the Cold War and the growing technical options available to terrorists. The collapse of Soviet hegemony over much of the Islamic world, coupled with the burgeoning wealth of the Muslim oil-producing countries, has given the Islamic world the freedom and means once again to support jihad around the globe. In short, the reason that the Umma are once again waging war against the non-Muslim world is because they can.

Naive or disingenuous commentators will point out that the five pillars of Islam—the religion's most basic doctrines—do not include anything about fighting non-Muslims. The five pillars of Islam are:

1. Faith (*iman*) in the oneness of God and the finality of the prophethood of Muhammad (indicated by the

declaration [the *Shahadah*] that, "There is no God but Allah and Muhammad is the messenger of Allah").

2. Keeping of the five scheduled daily prayers (*salah*).

3. Almsgiving (*zakat*).

4. Fasting (*sawm*) during the daylight hours of the lunar month of Ramadan.

5. Pilgrimage (*hajj*) to Mecca for those who are able.

It is usually not mentioned that jihad was once considered a sixth pillar of the faith. But whether jihad is actually a pillar or not, it is based directly on the teachings and exploits of Muhammad, a warlord directly responsible for the killing of hundreds, perhaps thousands, of people. Acknowledging the five pillars begs the question: What do Allah and Muhammad have in mind for Muslims? If the five pillars serve as the structure of the faith, what is its content? How is a Muslim to live out the teachings and example of the Prophet? The way that academics, politicians, and commentators pontificate about the "peaceful" ways of Islam without bothering to answer these basic questions constitutes an act of criminal intellectual negligence. A Muslim affirming that "Allah is my lord, Koran is my guide, *Sunnah* is my practice, jihad is my spirit, righteousness is my character, and paradise is my goal" sounds harmless enough to the ears of an unknowing Westerner. Only familiarity with the content of the Islamic sources themselves would permit one to grasp the violent implications of that seemingly innocuous statement of faith—a proclamation that just happens to be the creed of Hezbollah, one of the most notorious Islamic terrorist groups in the world.

Invariably, Islam's violent manifestations are qualified by Westerners with terms such as radical, extreme, fundamentalist, etc. This reflects a Western prejudice that anything that is violent is necessarily extreme or radical and that "authentic" religion is inherently pacific. Such a prejudice is the result of a Christian or Western-secular mind-set, which must be set aside when dealing with something that is decidedly outside Western tradition. It is instinctive for a Westerner to lump together virtues such as piety, faith, humility, sacrifice, love, and charity with nonviolence; the example of Christ, however much it is today explicitly accepted or rejected, has rooted such associations deep in the Western mind. In the Christian-Western tradition, violence is seen as pathological even if occasionally necessary; violence, and certainly killing for its own sake, is not a principle that enjoys widespread favor. In Islam, however, the virtues of piety, faith, humility, sacrifice, and charity go hand in hand with the violent struggle against the non-Islamic world in the quest of spreading the rule of Sharia law. While an observant Christian prays, gives alms, and turns the other cheek, an observant Muslim prays, gives alms, and wages war against the infidel whenever possible.

While it is necessary to distinguish between Muslims who commit and/or support acts of violence and those who do not, this distinction does not speak to the nature of Islam itself. There is no justification to assume that peaceable Muslims reflect "authentic" Islam while violent Muslims embrace an "extreme" variation. Rather, it is more accurate to speak of precisely what we see: peaceable Muslims and violent Muslims, without jumping to conclusions about which group is practicing authentic Islam. While terrorism is certainly extreme or radical from a Western viewpoint, this in no way implies that it is extreme from an Islamic one. Before we can assess the legitimacy or illegitimacy of Islamic violence, we must first understand Islam's own attitude toward violence—a no-brainer that has nonetheless managed to escape most "leading" Western minds.

The inadequacy of the contemporary analytical vocabulary is further illustrated by a few examples. Sayyid Qutb, a leading twentieth-century Muslim theorist, affirmed in his *Islam and Universal Peace* that Islam is indeed a religion of peace, and here is what he meant: Islam seeks the subjugation of the entire earth under Islamic law; when Islamic law becomes universally triumphant, peace will reign; therefore, Islam is a religion of peace. That the "peace" of Islam presupposes the destruction of non-Islamic civilization is surely more than a technical point to the infidel. A keen and pious man, there is no reason to doubt Qutb's sincerity.

Jihad was once understood in the West to mean "holy war," whereas now it is generally translated as "struggle." Indeed, struggle is the more literal translation; however, that struggle or "striving in the way of Allah," both in Muhammad's life and throughout Islamic history, has entailed organized violence against infidels and heretics. A word like "justice" implies the establishment of Sharia law and the eradication of non-Islamic legal, political, and religious systems. Islamic virtues such as "mercy," "forgiveness," "kindness," etc. apply toward other Muslims and (to a lesser degree) toward conquered, subservient peoples, but certainly not to mankind in general.

We often hear that Islam forbids suicide bombing. Indeed, the Koran does forbid suicide—but then we must ask the question: What is meant by suicide?

Sura 9:111. Verily, Allah has purchased of the believers their lives and their properties; for the price that theirs shall be the Paradise. They fight in Allah's Cause, so they kill (others) and are killed. It is a promise in truth which is binding on Him in the Tarot (Torah) and the Injeel (Gospel) and the Qur'an. And who is truer to his covenant than Allah? Then rejoice in the bargain which you have concluded. That is the supreme success.

It is this "kill others and are killed" that serves as the justification for what we call suicide bombing. "Suicide" bombing would indeed be forbidden by Islam—it's just that strapping explosives to oneself and wading into a crowd of infidels is not considered suicide but rather a legitimate act of jihad. While many Muslims dispute the tactical wisdom of suicide bombing, it is absurd to claim that there is any blanket Islamic proscription of it.

Let's take another example of the language problem: rape. Both the West and Islam forbid rape, but rape means very different things in the two societies. A broad Western definition of rape is any form of nonconsensual intercourse. In Islam, however, consent is not required of those women whom—in the language of the Koran—"one's right hand possesses" (Sura 33:52), that is, non-Muslim women captured during jihad. Captives of both sexes and all ages are legitimate plunder during jihad, the details of which are extensively outlined in the Koran and especially in Sura 8, entitled "War Booty." In addition to suffering the sexual assault itself, a rape victim in Muslim society often finds herself the target of an "honor" killing for having committed illicit fornication. It is Allah himself who instructs Muslims to stone adulterers, a practice enshrined by the Prophet Muhammad.

Because the current Western understanding of Islam is fraught with political correctitude, anachronistic concepts, and a totally inadequate vocabulary, we must develop a new conceptual framework. To do so, we must become acquainted with how Islam sees itself, and this in turn requires examination of those sources and authorities on which Islamic concepts, doctrines, practices, and history rest, namely, the Koran and the Sunnah. We must examine the revelations of the Koran and how they changed within Muhammad's lifetime from tolerance to intolerance; how Muhammad evolved from a persecuted preacher to a conquering warlord; and how Islam grew within Muhammad's lifetime from a simplified variation of other monotheistic religions to a blueprint for global political-military expansion. We will then be able to examine the history of Islam with an understanding of the motives and objectives of its adherents. The tremendous military campaigns waged by the Islamic empire in the first thousand years of its existence only make sense in light of the explicit instructions and precedents found in the Koran and the life of Muhammad. Having examined the theoretical and practical principles that underlie Islam's modus operandi, we will be able to make sense of the current state of the world and gauge what the future is likely to hold.

# PART II

# ISLAM SPEAKS

# 3

# THE KORAN

"As the Prophet is the messenger, the Quran is the message of God. Together they provide the basis for the ideal type of Muslim behaviour and thought . . . The Prophet himself had said in his last sermon: 'I leave behind me two things, the Quran and my example the Sunnah, and if you follow these you will never go astray.'"

—AKBAR S. AHMED[1]

ISLAMIC DOCTRINE DERIVES FROM TWO SOURCES: the Koran (or "recitation") and the Sunnah (or "way" of the Prophet Muhammad). The right-believing Muslim bases his beliefs and actions on the words of Allah as found in the Koran and on the precedents and teachings of the Prophet Muhammad. While the Koran is a single document, knowledge of the Sunnah comes from many different writings that provide Muslims with details about the life and teachings of Muhammad. The most important body of writings about Muhammad are the *hadiths* (or "reports" about Muhammad). Another text important to the study of the Sunnah is the *Sira* (the "life" of the Prophet), the canonical biography of Muhammad written by one of Islam's greatest scholars, Ibn Ishaq, in the eighth century. These documents—the Koran, the hadiths, and the Sira—provide the primary and near-exclusive sources of Islamic inspiration. (The other sources of Islamic inspiration are reason and consensus, but both of these hinge on, and defer to, the Koran and the Sunnah.) These sources reveal how Islam sees the world and what constitutes right conduct for Muslims on an individual and social level.

One of the problems that Westerners face when approaching the Islamic texts is that they are often ignorant of the rules that govern the Islamic interpretation of these sources. One such rule is abrogation, a principle that applies to the Koran (though some Islamic scholars apply it more broadly) in which passages that were revealed later in Muhammad's lifetime take priority over ones revealed earlier. There is also the critically important classification of hadiths into different levels of reliability. Without knowledge of the principle of abrogation, or which hadiths are considered reliable and which unreliable, understanding the meaning of the Islamic texts is impossible.

The Koran has no real parallel in the Western canon. According to Islamic orthodoxy, the Koran is the words of Allah verbatim. The Koran, in the Muslim view, was not inspired in the sense that many Christians view the Bible; rather the Koran is comparable to the stone tablets etched by the finger of Jehovah with the Ten Commandments on Mount Sinai. The *Cambridge Encyclopedia of Islam* even compares the Koran to Christ Himself, the "Word of God." Historically, there has existed a debate among Islamic scholars as to whether the Koran was created by Allah along with the rest of the universe or whether it existed for all time in uncreated form. Generally, Islamic orthodoxy teaches that the Koran has resided in heaven with Allah since before the creation of the universe and that it is perfect, unchanging, and incorruptible for all time. Following the creation of the world, the Koran was revealed through the Prophet Muhammad to humankind. The Koran's perfect and eternal nature gives the book an absolute preeminence and authority, which is why any tinkering with the text—or mishandling of the physical book itself—is an abomination. The idea of modifying or reinterpreting the Koran may be proposed by the occasional fringe scholar from time to time, but it is utterly anathema to orthodox Muslim sensibilities.

According to Islamic teaching, the Koran came down as a series of revelations from Allah through the Archangel Gabriel to the Prophet Muhammad who then dictated it to his followers. Muhammad's companions memorized fragments of the Koran and wrote them down on whatever was at hand. Some years after Muhammad's death these fragments were compiled into book form under the rule of Caliph Uthman, the third ruler of the Muslims after Muhammad.

I have used here a translation of the Koran by two Muslim scholars, Drs. Taqi-ud-Din Al-Hilali and Muhammad Muhsin Khan, which is much clearer to the non-Arabic reader than other translations.[2] Al-Hilali and Khan frequently include Arabic terms, which they explain parenthetically as opposed to confining themselves to a single best word. This approach helps the reader grasp the meaning of the original term in a general sense rather than relying on a single word chosen according to the personal preference of the translator. There are numerous Koranic translations by Muslims and non-Muslims available, and the reader is encouraged to have a look at them for himself, though some of the more recent versions have had their harsher passages whitewashed.

The Koran comprises 114 suras (or chapters) and is about as long as the Christian New Testament. According to Islamic doctrine, Muhammad received the first revelation from Allah through the Archangel Gabriel around AD 610 in a cave near the city of Mecca (now in southwest Saudi Arabia). The first revelation (Sura 96) commanded Muhammad to recite or read; the words he uttered were not his own but Allah's.

Over the next twelve years in Mecca, other revelations came to Muhammad that constituted a message to the inhabitants of the city to forsake their pagan ways and turn in worship to the one god, Allah.

While in Mecca, though he condemned paganism (for the most part), Muhammad showed respect for the monotheism of the Christian and Jewish inhabitants. Indeed, the Allah of the Koran claimed to be the same God worshipped by Jews and Christians, who now revealed himself to the Arab people through his chosen messenger, Muhammad. Muhammad claimed that the Jews and Christians, while "People of the Book" who possessed Abrahamic traditions of the one God, had distorted Allah's message and falsified their scriptures. Muhammad claimed to be the last prophet, the "seal" on prophecy that would reveal the errors of the Jews and Christians and restore Allah's preeminence on earth. The Koran speaks of biblical prophets and events, though it alters many biblical facts and timelines. While the Koranic revelations that came early in Muhammad's career in Mecca were generally benign, those that came later, after he and the first Muslims left Mecca for the city of Medina, were of a very different nature. It is these later revelations that transformed Islam into an expansionary, military-political ideology that perdures to this day.

It is difficult for a Westerner to develop a feel for the Koran because it originates from such a decidedly non-Western tradition. One sticking point is the doctrine that the Koran can never be translated from the Arabic. On several occasions, Allah makes clear that the Koran was revealed specifically in Arabic, for example:

> Sura 43:3. We verily, have made it a Koran in Arabic, that you may be able to understand (its meanings and its admonitions).

Consequently, orthodox Islam does not accept that a rendering of the Koran into another language is a translation in the way that, say, the King James Version is a translation of the original Greek and Hebrew Scriptures. A point often made by Islamic apologists to deflect criticism is to claim that only Arabic readers can understand the Koran and that non-Arabic speakers have no business looking into it in any way. But Arabic is a language like any other and is fully capable of translation. Indeed, most Muslims themselves are not Arabic readers.

> In other words, the majority of Muslims have to read the Koran in translation in order to understand it. . . . The Koran has now been translated into over a hundred languages, many of them by Muslims themselves, despite some sort of disapproval from the religious authorities.[3]

For religious purposes, the Koran must be *recited* in Arabic, but to be *understood* by most Muslims, who are not Arabic speakers, it must be translated.

As in the Jewish and Christian Scriptures, much of the Koran deals with the end of the world and the eternal fate of humankind. Suras 44 and 52 detail the Day of Judgment as well as heaven and hell, which are notably sensual in their character. Sinners are warned of "the Day when they will be pushed down by force to the Fire of Hell, with a horrible, forceful pushing" (Sura 52:13). Hell is filled with torments such as "boiling oil, it will boil in the bellies / Like the boiling of scalding water" (Sura 44:45-6), whereas in paradise, the righteous shall be married to "*Houris* (female fair ones) with wide, lovely eyes" (Sura 44:54; 52:20), "and there will go round boy-servants of theirs, to serve them as if they were preserved pearls" (Sura 52:24). The Koranic prohibition of alcohol will also be lifted (Sura 52:23).

Much of the Koran deals with "People of the Scripture" (or People of the Book), that is, Christians and Jews. Jesus is acknowledged by the Koran as a prophet of God but his divinity is rejected (Sura 4:171), which interestingly mirrors some early Christian heresies. The Crucifixion is also denied (Sura 4:157); Islam maintains no clear division between worldly and other-worldly power and so it cannot make sense of a prophet of God dying an ignominious death. Why would Allah, the all-powerful, all-wise, permit such a thing? The idea of a divine sacrifice freely given in order to restore fallen creation has no place in Islam. The Koran does mention a fall of sorts in its creation story, but it does not constitute a fundamental change in the relationship between Creator and created as does the sin of Genesis.

Without knowledge of the rule of abrogation to aid them in reading the Koran, Westerners are often left bewildered as to its meaning. The principle of abrogation—*al-naskh wa al-mansukh* ("the abrogating and the abrogated")—directs that verses revealed later in Muhammad's career abrogate—cancel and replace—earlier ones whose instructions they contradict.

Thus, passages revealed later in Muhammad's career, in Medina, overrule passages revealed earlier, in Mecca. The Koran itself lays out the principle of abrogation:

> Sura 2:106. Whatever a Verse (revelation) do We {Allah} abrogate or cause to be forgotten, We bring a better one or similar to it. Know you not that Allah is able to do all things?

It seems that Sura 2:106 was revealed in response to skepticism from Muhammad's detractors that Allah's revelations were not consistent over time. Muhammad's rebuttal was that "Allah is able to do all things"—even change his mind, and, indeed, Allah has made free use of this principle. Internal contradictions of the Koran are instantly reconciled through the rule that verses sent down by Allah later in Muhammad's career cancel and replace earlier verses with which they are inconsistent. Abrogation can be a difficult principle to grasp, especially in light of the doctrine that the Koran is eternal and unchanging. The abrogated verses have thus always existed as abrogated, even though they were authoritative in Muhammad's lifetime until later verses replaced them. For the purposes of our discussion we will have to set aside the peculiarity of this logic and merely note that there is no way to make sense of the Koran without the rule of abrogation.

But to confuse matters further, though the Koran was revealed to Muhammad over some twenty years' time, it was not compiled in chronological order. When the Koran was finally collated into book form, the suras were ordered from longest to shortest with no connection whatever to the order in which they were revealed or to their thematic content. In order to find out what the Koran says on a given topic, one must examine the other Islamic sources that give clues about when the revelations were received by Muhammad (see appendix II).

As one might expect, Islamic scholarship deals heavily with the question of which verses have been abrogated and which are still applicable. While there are different schools of thought on the precise effect of abrogation on the meaning of the Koran, there is general agreement on main points. One such point central to our exploration is that the various passages enjoining tolerance toward non-Muslims occurred early in Muhammad's career and have been overruled by later passages of a hostile nature. The earlier suras, revealed at a time when the Muslims were a small and vulnerable community in Mecca, are generally benign and tolerant; the later suras, revealed after Muhammad had made himself the head of an army in Medina, are bellicose and aggressive. In short, "all the passages recommending killing, decapitating, and maiming, the so-called 'Sword Verses,' are Medinan (i.e., later); 'tolerance' has been abrogated by 'intolerance.'"[4]

In the current public discourse on Islam, Muslim apologists cite ostensibly peaceful Koranic verses without acknowledging that those verses have been abrogated. The content of a Koranic passage is worth little if one doesn't know when it was revealed. Take for example Suras 50:45 and 109:1–6, both revealed in Mecca:

> Sura 50:45. We know of best what they say; and you (O Muhammad) are not a tyrant over them (to force them to Belief). But warn by the Qur'an, him who fears My Threat.

> Sura 109:1–6. Say (O Muhammad to these Mushrikun and Kafirun): "O Al-Kafirun (disbelievers in Allah, in His

Oneness, in His Angels, in His Books, in His Messengers, in the Day of Resurrection, and in Al-Qadar {divine foreordainment and sustaining of all things}, etc.)! I worship not that which you worship, nor will you worship that which I worship. And I shall not worship that which you are worshipping. Nor will you worship that which I worship. To you be your religion, and to me my religion (Islamic Monotheism)."

Live and let live is a theme in the earlier Meccan suras and it is easy to understand why. In Mecca, Muhammad found himself in a situation similar to that of many biblical prophets who were rejected and mocked by those around them. Fleeing to Medina to avoid probable assassination, his position improved only modestly. Both in Mecca and in their first days at Medina, the Muslims were a small and weak band who had to be careful not to antagonize the relatively powerful pagan establishment. Let us take this oft-cited passage:

> Sura 2:256. There is no compulsion in religion. Verily, the Right Path has become distinct from the wrong path. Whoever disbelieves in *Taghut* {idolatry} and believes in Allah, then he has grasped the most trustworthy handhold that will never break. And Allah is All-Hearer, All-Knower.

Sura 2 was one of the first revealed after the *Hijra* ("emigration" or "flight") from Mecca to Medina by Muhammad and his followers in AD 622. This revelation served to reassure the other Medinan tribes that the Muslims' intentions were benign. However, as Muhammad's position in Medina solidified and the Muslims developed a political and military presence, the Prophet began to reveal verses of an entirely different nature.

Some of the most violent passages in the Koran are to be found in the lengthy Sura 9, which according to some sources is either the last or next to last sura of the Koran to be revealed. Take for example, Sura 9:5, commonly called the "Verse of the Sword:"

> Sura 9:5. Then when the Sacred Months (the 1st, 7th, 11th, and 12th months of the Islamic calendar) have passed, then kill the *Mushrikun* {unbelievers} wherever you find them, and capture them and besiege them, and prepare for them each and every ambush. But if they repent and perform *As-Salat* (*Iqamat-as-Salat* {the Islamic ritual prayers}), and give Zakat {alms}, then leave their way free. Verily, Allah is Oft-Forgiving, Most Merciful.

The gist of the Verse of the Sword is plain: Allah commands that Muslims must fight non-Muslims until the latter are either killed or "repent" and perform the Islamic prayers and pay alms (i.e., become Muslims). The exhortations to violence in the Verse of the Sword abrogate the peaceful rhetoric of Suras 50:45, 109 and 2:256 because Sura 9 was revealed later in Muhammad's life.

Sura 8, also revealed in the later stage of Muhammad's life, reveals a similar theme:

> Sura 8:39. And fight them until there is no more *Fitnah* (disbelief and polytheism: i.e., worshipping others besides Allah) and the religion (worship) will all be for Allah Alone [in the whole of the world]. But if they cease (worshipping others besides Allah), then certainly, Allah is All-Seer of what they do.

> Sura 8:67. It is not for a Prophet that he should have prisoners of war (and free them with ransom) until he had made a great slaughter (among his enemies) in the land. You desire the good of this world (i.e., the money of ransom for freeing the captives), but Allah desires (for you) the Hereafter. And Allah is All Mighty, All-Wise.

Sura 9:29 allows for a third option for Jews and Christians (People of the Book). In lieu of death or conversion, People of the Book can live under submission to Islamic rule by paying the *jizya* (poll or head tax).

> Sura 9:29. Fight against those who believe not in Allah, nor in the Last Day, nor forbid that which has been forbidden by Allah and His Messenger and those who acknowledge not the religion of truth (i.e., Islam) among the people of the Scripture (Jews and Christians), until they pay the *Jizya* with willing submission, and feel themselves subdued.

> Sura 9:33. It is He {Allah} Who has sent His Messenger (Muhammad) with guidance and the religion of truth (Islam), to make it superior over all religions even though the *Mushrikun* (polytheists, pagans, idolaters, disbelievers in the Oneness of Allah) hate (it).

The Koran's commands to Muslims to wage war against non-Muslims in the name of Allah are unmistakable. Such commands are authoritative because they were revealed late in the Prophet's career and abrogate earlier instructions to coexist peaceably with infidels. Without knowledge of the principle of abrogation, Westerners will continue to misread the Koran on a fundamental level. Some, however, manage to misread the

Koran in a way that even knowledge of abrogation would not remedy. During his tenure as president, George W. Bush, for example, cited Sura 5:32 on at least two occasions to emphasize Islam's peacefulness:

> Sura 5:32. We ordained for the Children of Israel that if anyone killed a person not in retaliation of murder, or (and) to spread mischief in the land—it would be as if he killed all mankind, and if anyone saved a life, it would be as if he saved the life of all mankind. And indeed, there came to them Our Messengers with clear proofs, evidences, and signs, even then after that many of them continued to exceed the limits (e.g., by doing oppression unjustly and exceeding beyond the limits set by Allah by committing the major sins) in the land!

One expects that the President Bush's point would have come across somewhat differently had he not neglected to keep reading:

> Sura 5:33. The recompense of those who wage war against Allah and His Messenger and do mischief in the land is only that they shall be killed or crucified or their hands and their feet be cut off on the opposite sides, or be exiled from the land. That is their disgrace in this world, and a great torment is theirs in the Hereafter.

While the Koran's commands to kill and conquer unbelievers are plain, consultation of the other Islamic sources is necessary in order to fill in the details. The events, actions, teachings, and examples from the life of Muhammad constitute the Sunnah, the "way" of the Prophet, the second source of Islamic instruction in right belief and action.

Sura 59:7. And whatsoever the Messenger (Muhammad) gives you, take it, and whatsoever he forbids you, abstain (from it), and fear Allah. Verily, Allah is Severe in punishment.

As the man through whom the Koran was revealed and the "seal" of all the prophets, it is in the person of Muhammad that a Muslim discerns how to live a life faithful to his religion's tenets. Thus, it is to the teachings and example of the Prophet Muhammad that we now turn.

# 4

# THE SUNNAH

"It may be said that the Prophet is the perfection of both the norm of the human collectivity and the human individual, the norm for the perfect social life and the prototype and guide for the individual's spiritual life."

—SEYYED HOSSEIN[1]

ISLAM TEACHES THAT MUHAMMAD IS *AL-INSAN al-kamil* ("the ideal man"). Muhammad is in no way considered divine, nor is he worshipped (no image of Muhammad is permitted lest it encourage idolatry), but he is the model par excellence for all Muslims in how to conduct their lives. Muhammad's personal teachings and actions embody the Islamic ideal of a good and holy life. Details about the Prophet—how he lived, what he did, his non-Koranic utterances, his personal habits—are indispensable knowledge for any faithful Muslim.

Knowledge of the Sunnah comes primarily from the hadiths (reports) about Muhammad's life, which were passed down orally until codified in the eighth century AD, some one hundred years after Muhammad's death. The hadiths comprise the most important body of Islamic texts after the Koran. Hadiths are anecdotes about Muhammad's life believed to have originated with those who knew him personally. There are thousands of hadiths, some several pages long, some barely a few lines in length. When the hadiths were first compiled in the eighth century, it became obvious that many were inauthentic. By examining the chain of oral transmitters (*isnads*) through which a given hadith had been passed, early Muslim scholars made determinations as to a given hadith's reliability. Those hadiths found to possess the highest reliability were classified as *sahih* (sound or reliable). These *sahih* hadiths (reliable reports) serve as the primary means for studying the Sunnah.

The hadiths we shall examine come exclusively from the most reliable and authoritative collection, *Sahih Al-Bukhari*, recognized as reliable by all schools of Islamic scholarship, in this case translated and categorized by Dr. Muhammad Muhsin Khan.[2] As usual, all parenthetical explanations in the text are those of the translator except for my interjections in braces, { }. Different translations of hadiths can vary in their breakdown of volume, book, and number, but the content is the same. For each hadith, the classifying information is listed first (Volume, Book, Number), then the name of the narrator of the hadith (generally someone who knew Muhammad personally), and then the content itself. Sometimes the narrator of a hadith will refer to himself or to a third party along with a reference to the Prophet.

As the ideal man and final prophet of God, nothing about Muhammad is irrelevant to Islamic orthodoxy, and so many hadiths include information that to a Westerner might seem mundane, petty, or even bizarre. For example:

Volume 1, Book 3, Number 134. *Narrated Ali:* I used to get the emotional urethral discharge frequently so I requested

Al Miqdad to ask the Prophet about it. Al-Miqdad asked him and he replied, "One has to perform ablution (after it)."

Volume 1, Book 4, Number 151. *Narrated Abdullah bin Umar:* Once I went up the roof of our house and saw Allah's Apostle answering the call of nature while sitting over two bricks facing Bait-ul-Maqdis (Jerusalem).

That these sorts of anecdotes from Muhammad's life are passed down as important religious teachings to this day testifies to the truly alien quality of Islam from a Western standpoint.

Because Muhammad is himself the measuring stick of morality, his actions are not judged according to an independent moral standard but rather establish what the proper standard of morality for Muslims is. This fact lends to many hadiths an impassive, almost clinical tone notwithstanding the nature of the content.

Volume 7, Book 62, Number 88. *Narrated Ursa:* The Prophet wrote the (marriage contract) with Aisha while she was six years old and consummated his marriage with her while she was nine years old and she remained with him for nine years (i.e., till his death).

Volume 8, Book 82, Number 795. *Narrated Anas:* The Prophet cut off the hands and feet of the men belonging to the tribe of Uraina and did not cauterise (their bleeding limbs) till they died.

That a middle-aged man should marry and have sexual relations with a nine-year-old girl or that he should dismember people and leave them to die are not, in the case of Muhammad and his religion, sins to be condemned but moral precedents to be followed. Other hadiths establish explicit legal precedents for right conduct in Islamic society, including punishments for various offenses.

> Volume 2, Book 23, Number 413. *Narrated Abdullah bin Umar:* The Jews {of Medina} brought to the Prophet a man and a woman from amongst them who have {sic} committed (adultery) illegal sexual intercourse. He ordered both of them to be stoned (to death), near the place of offering the funeral prayers beside the mosque.

> Volume 9, Book 84, Number 57. *Narrated 'Ikrima:* Some *Zanadiqa* (atheists) were brought to Ali {the fourth Caliph} and he burnt them. The news of this event, reached Ibn Abbas who said, "If I had been in his place, I would not have burnt them, as Allah's Apostle forbade it, saying, 'Do not punish anybody with Allah's punishment (fire).' I would have killed them according to the statement of Allah's Apostle, 'Whoever changes his Islamic religion, then kill him.'"

The stoning of adulterers and execution of apostates continues to this day in Muslim countries throughout the world, sometimes carried out officially, other times by self-proclaimed Islamic authorities or the families of the offenders.

As with much of the Koran, many hadiths deal with the Prophet's considerable political and military exploits. These hadiths reveal the bloody environment in which Islam developed and that shapes its worldview to this day. On numerous occasions Muhammad makes clear the virtue and necessity of physical combat for Muslims.

Volume 1, Book 2, Number 25. *Narrated Abu Huraira:* Allah's Apostle was asked, "What is the best deed?" He replied, "To believe in Allah and His Apostle (Muhammad)." The questioner then asked, "What is the next (in goodness)? He replied, "To participate in Jihad (religious fighting) in Allah's Cause."

In contrast to the Bible—a compilation of many books composed by various persons over the course of centuries—the Islamic holy texts all devolve directly from the life of one man. In Islam, there is no natural sense of morality or justice that transcends the specific examples and injunctions outlined in the Koran and the Sunnah. Because Muhammad is considered Allah's final prophet and the Koran is believed to be the eternal, unalterable words of Allah himself, the entire Islamic moral universe devolves solely from the life and teachings of Muhammad. To understand the Islamic view of the world, we must come to grips with the story of Muhammad himself: who he was, what he taught, and what he did. Only then will the conduct and motivation of faithful Muslims who seek to model their lives after Muhammad come into focus.

## THE "LIFE OF THE PROPHET OF GOD"

A further source of information about Muhammad is the *Sira* (life), a biography of the Prophet composed by one of Islam's greatest scholars, Muhammad ibn Ishaq, in the eighth century. Along with the Koran and the reliable hadiths, the Sira is a principal text of the Islamic faith.[3] Thanks to the Sira, we have a narrative biography of Muhammad that clarifies a great deal about this man, one of the most consequential figures in world history.

According to the Islamic sources, Muhammad was born in Mecca in AD 570 and spent the first decades of his adult life as a merchant in his native city. He married his first wife, Khadija, some fifteen years his senior, when he was about twenty-five. Though an orphan, Muhammad was a member of the prestigious Quraish tribe and enjoyed the protection of his powerful uncle, Abu Talib.

Muhammad's prophetic career is meaningfully divided into two segments: the first in Mecca, where he labored for fourteen years to make converts to Islam, and the second in the city of Medina (the "City of the Apostle of God"), where he became a powerful political and military leader. In Mecca, we see a quasi-biblical figure preaching repentance and charity, harassed and rejected by those around him. Later, in Medina, we see an able commander and strategist who systematically conquered and killed those who opposed him. It is the later years of Muhammad's life in Medina, from AD 622 to his death in 632, that are rarely discussed in polite company.

In 622, when the Prophet was more than fifty years old, he and his followers made the Hijra (emigration or flight) from Mecca to the oasis of Yathrib (later renamed Medina) some two hundred miles to the north. Muhammad's new monotheism had angered the pagan leaders of Mecca, and the flight to Medina was precipitated by a probable attempt on Muhammad's life. Muhammad had sent emissaries to Medina to ensure his welcome. He was accepted by the Medinan tribes as the leader of the Muslims and as an arbiter of intertribal disputes. At Medina, Muhammad began the establishment of a political-military community amongst the other tribes, many of them Jewish. Before the Hijra, Muhammad's teachings and actions in Mecca could be said to be loosely compatible with Christian and modern secular standards of behavior and communal organization. In Medina, the picture changed radically.

Shortly before Muhammad fled the hostility of Mecca, a new batch of Muslim converts pledged their loyalty to him on a hill outside Mecca called Aqaba. The Sira conveys the significance of this event:

> Sira, page 208. When God gave permission to his Apostle to fight, the second {oath of allegiance at} Aqaba contained conditions involving war which were not in the first act of fealty. Now they {Muhammad's followers} bound themselves to war against all and sundry for God and his Apostle, while he promised them for faithful service thus the reward of paradise.

> Sira, pages 212–13. The Apostle had not been given permission to fight or allowed to shed blood before the second {oath of allegiance at} Aqaba. He had simply been ordered to call men to God and to endure insult and forgive the ignorant. . . . The first [Koranic] verse which was sent down on this subject was: "Permission is given to those who fight because they have been wronged." {Sura 22:40} Then God sent down to him: "Fight them so that there be no more seduction," i.e., until no believer is seduced from his religion. "And the religion is God's," i.e., until God alone is worshipped {Sura 2:198}.

That Islam underwent a dramatic change at this point in Muhammad's life is plain. The Sira's author clearly intends to impress on his Muslim readers that, while in its early years Islam might have been a tolerant creed that would "endure insult and forgive the ignorant," Allah soon required Muslims "to war against all and sundry for God and his Apostle." The Islamic calendar testifies to the paramouncy of the Hijra by setting year one from the date of its occurrence. The year of the Hijra, AD 622, is considered more significant than the year of Muhammad's birth or death or that of the first Koranic revelation because Islam is first and foremost a political-military enterprise. Islam achieved its proper political-military articulation only when Muhammad left Mecca with his paramilitary band. The years of the Islamic calendar (which uses lunar months) are designated in English "AH" or "After Hijra."

While he had remained in Mecca, Muhammad was a member of the leading Quraish tribe, but few of his fellow tribesmen accepted his religion. Indeed, the Quraish of Mecca became Muhammad's sharpest detractors and precipitated his emigration to Medina. The major battles later waged by Muhammad were directed largely against Quraish power. According to the Sira (pages 659–60), the Muslims under Muhammad engaged in some eighty-four battles and raids between AD 622 and 632. Muhammad was present for twenty-seven of these and personally fought in nine. Four engagements, however, stand out: the battles of Badr, Uhud, Medina (or the Battle of the Trench), and Mecca. Details of these battles illuminate the essential nature of violence in Islam and provide orthodox Muslims with a blueprint for their own conduct.

## BATTLE OF BADR
The Battle of Badr was the first significant engagement fought by the Prophet. Upon establishing himself in Medina following the Hijra, Muhammad began a series of *razzias* (raids) on Quraish caravans on the route between Mecca and Syria. Raiding became

the principle means of sustenance for the Muslims, to whom the agricultural society of Medina was foreign. According to the Islamic sources, Muhammad was not seeking a genuine battle at Badr—an oasis west of Medina—but rather hoping to plunder what he had heard was an especially rich caravan heading south to Mecca.

> Volume 5, Book 59, Number 287. *Narrated Kab bin Malik:* The Apostle had gone out to meet the caravans of Quraish, but Allah caused them (i.e., Muslims) to meet their enemy unexpectedly (with no previous intention).

The Muslims abruptly found themselves confronted with an armed force of some three times their strength. Despite the unfavorable odds, Muhammad expressed great confidence to his old friend and father-in-law, Abu Bakr, who would later succeed the Prophet as first Caliph.

> Volume 5, Book 59, Number 289. *Narrated Ibn Abbas:* On the day of the battle of Badr, the Prophet said, "O Allah! I appeal to You (to fulfill) Your Covenant and Promise. O Allah! If Your Will is that none should worship You (then give victory to the pagans)." Then Abu Bakr took hold of him by the hand and said, "This is sufficient for you." The Prophet came out saying, "Their multitude will be put to flight and they will show their backs." (Sura 54:45)

As Muhammad's prayer before Badr indicates, defeat of the Muslims in battle would amount to defeat of Allah's religion. It is this simple equation of the spiritual and the worldly that sanctifies Muslim violence to this day. Though outnumbered, the Muslims defeated the Quraish, a victory which consolidated

Muhammad's position as a prophet and commander. As the hadiths describing Badr indicate, the Meccan Quraish tribe were not to be considered worthy men fighting in a legitimate cause (the protection of the fruits of their labor) to whom their victors ought to extend mercy and goodwill; rather, they were enemies of God who, by defying Muhammad, defied Allah himself. Gabriel, the messenger of Allah who brought Muhammad the Koranic revelations, informed the Prophet that Allah had sent his angels to assist in the fighting, which confirmed that the Muslims were fighting in a sacred cause though their principal aim was to raid a caravan.

After the Battle of Badr, Allah sent down Sura 8, *Anfal* (War Booty) almost in its entirety, comprising seventy five verses and which is one of the longest suras in the Koran. The meaning of Sura 8 is revealed by its context (i.e., the first battle between Muslims and infidels).

> Sura 8:1-6. They ask you (O Muhammad) about the spoils of war. Say: "The spoils are for Allah and the Messenger." So fear Allah and adjust all matters of difference among you, and obey Allah and His Messenger (Muhammad), if you are believers. The believers are only those who, when Allah is mentioned, feel a fear in their hearts and when His Verses (this Qur'an) are recited unto them, they (i.e., the Verses) increase their Faith; and they put their trust in their Lord (Alone); Who perform As-Salat (Iqamat-as-Salat {the Islamic prayers}) and spend out of that We have provided them. It is they who are the believers in truth. For them are grades of dignity with their Lord, and Forgiveness and a generous provision (Paradise). As your Lord caused you (O Muhammad) to go out from your

home with the truth, and verily, a party among the believers disliked it; Disputing with you concerning the truth after it was made manifest, as if they were being driven to death, while they were looking (at it).

Sura 8:15-20. O you who believe! When you meet those who disbelieve, in a battle-field, never turn your backs to them. And whoever turns his back to them on such a day—unless it be a stratagem of war, or to retreat to a troop (of his own),—he indeed has drawn upon himself wrath from Allah. And his abode is Hell, and worst indeed is that destination! You killed them not, but Allah killed them. And you (Muhammad) threw not when you did throw but Allah threw, that He might test the believers by a fair trial from Him. Verily, Allah is All-Hearer, All Knower. This (is the fact) and surely, Allah weakens the deceitful plots of the disbelievers. (O disbelievers) if you ask for a judgment, now has the judgment come unto you and if you cease (to do wrong), it will be better for you, and if you return (to the attack), so shall we return, and your forces will be of no avail to you, however numerous it be, and verily, Allah is with the believers. O you who believe! Obey Allah and His Messenger, and turn not away from him (i.e., Messenger Muhammad) while you are hearing.

The themes found in Sura 8 are oft-repeated throughout the Islamic holy texts: individual Muslims may prefer the safer path of not fighting, but Allah himself desires that they participate in combat; Allah fights on behalf of Muslims, so they must not be cowed by a stronger opponent; to eschew combat is to court eternal damnation; individual Muslims are not responsible for the killing of others in battle because it is Allah who in fact kills their enemies; and, finally, obey Muhammad in all things.

Returning to Medina victorious after Badr, Muhammad admonished the resident Jewish tribe of Bani Qaynuqa to accept Islam or face a similar fate as the Quraish (Sura 3:12–13). The Bani Qaynuqa was the first of three Jewish tribes to be subjugated by Muhammad. The Bani Qaynuqa took refuge in their fortresses outside Medina but eventually succumbed to the Muslims' siege when the other Medinan tribes failed to render them assistance. Whether in a spirit of genuine leniency or because he was at this time too weak to press his advantage, Muhammad granted the Bani Qaynuqa a conditional surrender and permitted them to depart from Medina with their armor and possessions. Muhammad thus bloodlessly removed a competitor from the Medinan polity. The Jewish tribes in particular were a source of rivalry because, like Muhammad, they claimed to possess the definitive religion of the one god. Muhammad endeavored to convince the Jews that he was a prophet in their own tradition, but he met with little success.

> Sura 5:57. O you who believe! Take not for *Auliya* (protectors and helpers) those who take your religion for a mockery and fun from among those who received the Scripture (Jews and Christians) before you, nor from among the disbelievers; and fear Allah if you indeed are true believers.

> Sura 5:60. Say (O Muhammad to the people of the Scripture): "Shall I inform you of something worse than that, regarding the recompense from Allah: those (Jews) who incurred the Curse of Allah and His Wrath, those of whom (some) He transformed into monkeys and swine, those who worshipped

*Taghut* (false deities); such are worse in rank (on the Day of Resurrection in the Hell-fire), and far more astray from the Right Path (in the life of this world)."

Following the exile of the Bani Qaynuqa, Muhammad turned his attention to individuals in Medina he believed to have acted treacherously toward Islam. The Prophet especially disliked the many poets who ridiculed his new religion and his claim to prophethood—a theme that recurs today in the violent reactions of some Muslims to any perceived mockery of Islam. In taking action against his opponents, "the ideal man" set precedents for all time as to how Muslims should deal with detractors of their religion.

> Sira, page 367. Then he {Kab bin al-Ashraf} composed amatory verses of an insulting nature about the Muslim women. The Apostle said . . . "Who will rid me of Ibnul-Ashraf?" Muhammad bin Maslama, brother of the Bani Abdu'l-Ashhal, said, "I will deal with him for you, O Apostle of God, I will kill him." He said, "Do so if you can." . . . "All that is incumbent upon you is that you should try" {said the Prophet to Muhammad bin Maslama}. He said, "O Apostle of God, we shall have to tell lies." He {the Prophet} answered, "Say what you like, for you are free in the matter."

> Volume 4, Book 52, Number 270. *Narrated Jabir bin Abdullah:* The Prophet said, "Who is ready to kill Kab bin Al-Ashraf who has really hurt Allah and His Apostle?" Muhammad bin Maslama said, "O Allah's Apostle! Do you like me to kill him?" He replied in the affirmative. So, Muhammad bin Maslama went to him (i.e., Kab) and said,

"This person (i.e., the Prophet) has put us to task and asked us for charity." Kab replied, "By Allah, you will get tired of him." Muhammad said to him, "We have followed him, so we dislike to leave him till we see the end of his affair." Muhammad bin Maslama went on talking to him in this way till he got the chance to kill him.

A significant portion of the Sira is devoted to poetry composed by Muhammad's followers and his enemies in rhetorical duels that mirrored those in the field. There seems to have been an informal competition in aggrandizing oneself, one's tribe, and one's god while ridiculing one's adversary in eloquent and memorable ways. This is what got Kab bin al-Ashraf into trouble.

> Sira, page 368. Kab bin Malik said: of them Kab was left prostrate there. (After his fall {the Jewish tribe of} al-Nadir were brought low). Sword in hand we cut him down by Muhammad's order when he sent secretly by night Kab's brother to go to Kab. He beguiled him and brought him down with guile Mahmud was trustworthy, bold.

Shortly thereafter, Muhammad gave explicit instructions: "The Apostle said, 'Kill any Jew that falls into your power'" (Sira, page 369). With Muhammad as their exemplar, the wonder today is not that so many Muslims are violent but that so many are peaceful.

## BATTLE OF UHUD

Following their stinging defeat at Badr and the loss of many of their young nobles, the Meccan Quraish regrouped for an attack on the Muslims at Medina. Muhammad got wind of the

Meccan force coming to attack him and encamped his forces on a small hillock north of Medina named Uhud, where the ensuing battle took place.

> Volume 5, Book 59, Number 377. *Narrated Jabir bin Abdullah:* On the day of the battle of Uhud, a man came to the Prophet and said, "Can you tell me where I will be if I should get martyred?" The Prophet replied, "In Paradise." The man threw away some dates he was carrying in his hand, and fought till he was martyred.

Muhammad gave his troops specific instructions as to how to fight the battle. In particular, he instructed his archers not to be drawn into the fight no matter what happened. The Muslims' greed, however, got the better of them and they rushed after the fleeing Quraish women at a critical moment.

> Volume 5, Book 59, Number 375. *Narrated Al-Bara:* When we faced the enemy, they took to their heel till I saw their women running towards the mountain, lifting up their clothes from their legs, revealing their leg-bangles. The Muslims started saying, "The booty, the booty!" Abdullah bin Jubair said, "The Prophet had taken a firm promise from me not to leave this place." But his companions refused (to stay). So when they refused (to stay there), (Allah) confused them so that they could not know where to go, and they suffered seventy casualties.

Thanks to the Muslims' lack of discipline, the battle at Uhud ended as a draw and both sides disengaged.

Sira, page 391. The day of Uhud was a day of trial, calamity, and heart-searching on which God tested the believers and put the hypocrites on trial, those who professed faith with their tongue and hid unbelief in their hearts; and a day in which God honoured with martyrdom those whom he willed.

Perhaps the most enduring lesson from the recounts of Uhud (and Muhammad's military career generally) for orthodox Muslims is Allah's disdain for those who seek the safety and comforts of home rather than the fire of battle.

Sura 2:216. Jihad (holy fighting in Allah's cause) is ordained for you (Muslims) though you dislike it, and it may be that you dislike a thing which is good for you and that you like a thing which is bad for you. Allah knows but you do not know.

Sura 9:41–45. March forth, whether you are light (being healthy, young, and wealthy) or heavy (being ill, old, and poor), strive hard with your wealth and your lives in the Cause of Allah. This is better for you, if you but knew. Had it been a near gain (booty in front of them) and an easy journey, they would have followed you [O Muhammad], but the distance (Tabuk expedition {a raiding expedition}) was long for them, and they would swear by Allah, "If we only could, we would certainly have come forth with you." They destroy their ownselves, and Allah knows that they are liars. May Allah forgive you (O Muhammad). Why did you grant them leave (for remaining behind, you should have persisted as regards your order to them to proceed on Jihad), until those who told the truth were seen by you in a clear light, and you had known the liars? Those who believe in Allah and the Last Day would not ask your leave to be exempted from fighting with their properties and their lives, and Allah is the All-Knower of *Al-Muttaqun* (the pious). It is only those who believe not in Allah and the Last Day and whose hearts are in doubt that ask your leave (to be exempted from Jihad). So in their doubts they waver.

In Sura 9:44–45 we find an important standard for distinguishing true Muslims from those who pay Allah mere lip service: when called upon to do so, the true believers are ready to sacrifice themselves and their possessions in battle but the faithless seek exemption from fighting.

> Sura 61:4. Verily, Allah loves those who fight in His Cause in rows (ranks) as if they were a solid structure.

> Volume 4, Book 52, Number 50. *Narrated Anas bin Malik:* The Prophet said, "A single endeavor (of fighting) in Allah's Cause in the forenoon or in the afternoon is better than the world and whatever is in it."

Though deprived of victory at Uhud, Muhammad was by no means vanquished. He continued making raids that made being a Muslim not only virtuous in the eyes of Allah but lucrative as well. In an Islamic worldview, there is no incompatibility between wealth, power, and holiness. Indeed, as a member of the true faith, it is only logical that one should also enjoy the material bounty of Allah—even if that means stealing it from infidels.

As Muhammad had neutralized the Jewish tribe of Bani Qaynuqa after the Battle of Badr, he now turned to the Jewish Bani Nadir after the Battle of Uhud. According to the Sira, Allah warned Muhammad of an attempt to assassinate him, and the

Prophet ordered the Muslims to prepare for war against the Bani Nadir. Like the Bani Qaynuqa, the Bani Nadir withdrew into a series of forts outside Medina. As the siege dragged on, Muhammad ordered the outlying date trees of the Bani Nadir destroyed. As before, none of the other Medinan tribes came to the aid of their besieged fellows. The Bani Nadir agreed to go into exile if Muhammad permitted them to retain their movable property. Muhammad agreed to these terms save that they leave behind their armor. Slowly but surely Muhammad was eliminating possible threats from within Medina and consolidating his position atop its political hierarchy.

## BATTLE OF MEDINA

In AD 627, some five years after the Hijra, Muhammad faced the greatest challenge to his new community. In that year, the Quraish of Mecca made their most determined attack on the Muslims at Medina itself. The Quraish had assembled a very large force, in the neighborhood of fourteen-hundred mounted men. Given their numbers, Muhammad thought it advisable not to engage them in a pitched battle as at Uhud but took shelter in Medina, protected as it was by lava flows on three sides. The Meccans would have to attack from the northwest in a valley between the flows, and it was there that Muhammad ordered a trench dug for the city's defense. In the ensuing battle, many recent converts to Islam joined Muhammad and those who had emigrated with him from Mecca in preparing and manning the trench.

Volume 4, Book 52, *Number 208. Narrated Anas:* On the day (of the battle) of the Trench, the *Ansar* {allies of the Muslims} were saying, "We are those who have sworn allegiance to Muhammad for Jihad (for ever) as long as we live." The Prophet replied to them, "O Allah! There is no life except the life of the Hereafter. So honor the *Ansar* and {the original} emigrants {from Mecca} with Your Generosity."

*And Narrated Mujashi:* My brother and I came to the Prophet and I requested him to take the pledge of allegiance from us for migration. He said, "Migration has passed away with its people." I asked, "For what will you take the pledge of allegiance from us then?" He said, "I will take (the pledge) for Islam and Jihad."

The trench foiled the Meccans, who were only able to send small raiding parties across it. After several days' standoff, worn out from exposure and lack of food, the Meccans ignominiously turned back for home. The Battle of Medina (or the Trench) marked the beginning of a rapid decline of Quraish power. From then on, Muhammad's star was clearly in the ascendant and his preeminence in Arabia was never seriously challenged again. Muhammad's superior tactics and the ensuing humiliation of the Meccans were interpreted by the Muslims as further signs of Allah's favor, which expunged the lack of victory at Uhud. After the Battle of the Trench, the exhausted Prophet appears to have believed that his "striving in the way of Allah" was completed for the time being, but he was wrong.

Volume 4, Book 52, Number 68. *Narrated Aisha:* When Allah's Apostle returned on the day (of the battle) of Al-Khandaq (i.e., Trench), he put down his arms and took a bath. Then {Archangel} Gabriel whose head was covered with dust, came to him saying, "You have put down your arms! By Allah, I have not put down my arms yet." Allah's Apostle said, "Where (to go now)?" Gabriel said, "This way," pointing towards the tribe of Bani Quraiza. So Allah's Apostle went out towards them.

Now the third Jewish tribe at Medina, the Bani Quraiza, were to suffer Muhammad's displeasure. While the Bani Qaynuqa and Bani Nadir suffered only exile, the fate of the Bani Quraiza would be considerably more dire. Having received instructions from Gabriel about the Bani Quraiza, "The Apostle besieged them for twenty-five nights until they were sore pressed and God cast terror into their hearts" (Sira, page 461). The Bani Quraiza finally surrendered to the Prophet, who placed their fate in the hands of a recent convert wounded at the Battle of the Trench, Sad bin Muadh.

> Volume 5, Book 59, Number 448. *Narrated Aisha:* They {the tribe of Quraiza} then surrendered to the Prophet's judgment but he directed them to Sad to give his verdict concerning them. Sad said, "I give my judgment that their warriors should be killed, their women and children should be taken as captives, and their properties distributed."

> Sira, pages 463–64. Then they {the tribe of Quraiza} surrendered, and the apostle confined them in Medina in the quarter of d. al Harith, a woman of Bani al-Najjar. Then the apostle went out to the market of Medina and dug trenches in it. Then he sent for them and struck off their heads in those trenches as they were brought out to him in batches. Among them was the enemy of Allah Huyayy bin Akhtab

and Kab bin Asad their chief. There were 600 or 700 in all, though some put the figure as high as 800 or 900. As they were being taken out in batches to the Apostle they asked Kab what he thought would be done with them. He replied, "Will you never understand? Don't you see that the summoner never stops and those who are taken away do not return? By Allah it is death!" This went on until the Apostle made an end of them.

Here we find the clear precedent that explains the peculiar penchant of Islamic terrorists (and some governments such as Saudi Arabia) to behead their victims: it is merely another precedent bestowed by their Prophet. Beheading has a Koranic basis as well:

Sura 47:4. So, when you meet (in fight Jihad in Allah's Cause), those who disbelieve smite at their necks till when you have killed and wounded many of them, then bind a bond firmly (on them, i.e., take them as captives). Thereafter (is the time) either for generosity (i.e., free them without ransom), or ransom (according to what benefits Islam), until the war lays down its burden. Thus [you are ordered by Allah to continue in carrying out Jihad against the disbelievers till they embrace Islam, (i.e., are saved from the punishment in the Hell-fire) or at least come under your protection], but if it had been Allah's Will, He Himself could certainly have punished them (without you). But (He lets you fight), in order to test you, some with others. But those who are killed in the Way of Allah, He will never let their deeds be lost.

In Sura 47:4 we learn that, in addition to Allah's desire that Islam reign supreme on earth, the actual fighting itself is a test from Allah, which believers shirk at their peril. The Koran also teaches that jihad is really a charitable act bestowed upon unbelievers that grants them Muslim "protection" and even delivers them from perdition—even though it means making war against them.

Following the massacre of the Bani Quraiza, Muhammad turned to eliminating individuals in Medina whom he believed had sown treachery among the other Medinan tribes.

> Sira, page 482. When the fight at the trench and the affair of Bani Quraiza were over, the matter of Sallam bin Abu'l-Huqayq known as Abu Rafi came up in connexion with those who had collected the mixed tribes together against the Apostle.

> Volume 4, Book 52, Number 264. *Narrated Al-Bara bin Azib:* Allah's Apostle sent a group of Ansari men to kill Abu-Rafi. One of them set out and entered their (i.e., the enemies') fort. That man said, "I hid myself in a stable for their animals. They closed the fort gate. Later they lost a donkey of theirs, so they went out in its search. I, too, went out along with them, pretending to look for it. They found the donkey and entered their fort. And I, too, entered along with them. They closed the gate of the fort at night, and kept its keys in a small window where I could see them. When those people slept, I took the keys and opened the gate of the fort and came upon Abu Rafi and said, 'O Abu Rafi.' When he replied, I proceeded towards the voice and hit him. He shouted and I came out to come back, pretending to be a

helper. I said, 'O Abu Rafi,' changing the tone of my voice. He asked me, 'What do you want; woe to your mother?' I asked him, 'What has happened to you?' He said, 'I don't know who came to me and hit me.' Then I drove my sword into his belly and pushed it forcibly till it touched the bone. Then I came out, filled with puzzlement and went towards a ladder of theirs in order to get down but I fell down and sprained my foot. I came to my companions and said, 'I will not leave till I hear the wailing of the women.' So, I did not leave till I heard the women bewailing Abu Rafi, the merchant of Hijaz. Then I got up, feeling no ailment, (and we proceeded) till we came upon the Prophet and informed him."

What is even more striking than the vividness of the above account is that it was recorded so meticulously and passed down through the centuries. It is one thing for the assassination to have taken place in the way that it did, and it is one thing to record the fact of the killing, but it is something else entirely to set out the gory details for the edification of posterity with such painful explicitness. Yet another precedent for the Islamic faithful.

Sira, pages 483–84. God, what a fine band you met, O Ibnul-Huqayq and Ibnul Ashraf! They went to you with sharp swords, brisk as lions in a tangled thicket, until they came on you in your dwelling and made you drink death with their swift-slaying swords, looking for the victory of their Prophet's religion, despising every risk of hurt.

The unmistakable message is that killing for Allah is a virtuous enterprise that warrants the laudation of the perpetrator and the enshrinement of the deed in collective memory. It is not hard to see where today's Islamic terrorists derive their inspiration.

Following the slaughter of the Quraiza, Muhammad embarked on a new series of raids against neighboring tribes. One such raid brought the Muslims up against the exiled Jewish tribe of Bani Nadir, who had settled in a place called Khaibar. An incident involving a female captive lends insight into the Islamic view of women. Islam shows little regard for the lives of infidels, and it similarly cares little for the welfare of women.

Volume 1, Book 8, Number 367. *Narrated Abdul Aziz:* When he {Muhammad} entered the town, he said, "*Allahu Akbar!* Khaibar is ruined. Whenever we approach near a (hostile) nation (to fight) then evil will be the morning of those who have been warned." He repeated this thrice. The people came out for their jobs and some of them said, "Muhammad (has come)." (Some of our companions added, "With his army.") We conquered Khaibar, took the captives, and the booty was collected. Dihya came and said, "O Allah's Prophet! Give me a slave girl from the captives." The Prophet said, "Go and take any slave girl." He took Safiya bin Huyai. A man came to the Prophet and said, "O Allah's Apostles! You gave Safiya bin Huyai to Dihya and she is the chief mistress of the tribes of Quraiza and An-Nadir and she befits none but you." So the Prophet said, "Bring him along with her." So Dihya came with her and when the Prophet saw her, he said to Dihya, "Take any slave girl other than her from the captives." Anas added: "The Prophet then manumitted her and married her."

Volume 5, Book 59, Number 523. Narrated Anas bin Malik: The Prophet stayed with Safiya bin Huyai for three days on the way of Khaibar where he consummated his marriage with her. Safiya was amongst those who were ordered to use a veil.

Sira, page 511. The women of Khaibar were distributed among the Muslims.

In seventh century Arabic tribal culture, women were seen as commodities to be bought, sold, or otherwise appropriated as one was able, an attitude that Islam has perpetuated. The hapless slave girl Safiya appears as little more than a prestigious trophy to be haggled over and traded at the will of the victors. It is this same mentality that gave rise to the Muslim rape epidemic that has plagued major cities in Sweden and Norway, in which Muslims routinely attack unveiled native women.[4] The fate of her husband, Kinana, renders Safiya's plight even more disturbing:

Sira, page 515. Kinana bin al-Rabi, who had the custody of the treasure of Bani al-Nadir, was brought to the Apostle who asked him about it. He denied that he knew where it was. A Jew came to the Apostle and said that he had seen Kinana going round a certain ruin every morning early. When the Apostle said to Kinana, "Do you know that if we find you have it I shall kill you?" he said, "Yes." The Apostle gave orders that the ruin was to be excavated and some of the treasure was found. When he asked him about the rest he refused to produce it, so the Apostle gave orders to al-Zubayr bin al-Awwam, "Torture him until you extract what he has," so he kindled a fire with flint and steel on his chest until he was nearly dead. Then the Apostle delivered him to Muhammad bin Maslama and he struck off his head, in revenge for his brother Mahmud.

Muhammad besieged Khaibar until the Bani Nadir surrendered on the condition that he spare their lives. The nearby people of Faduk got wind of the surrender and sent an emissary to Muhammad requesting similar terms. Muhammad agreed to permit them to continue farming their land provided they hand over half of the produce to the Muslims—with the important condition that "if we wish to expel you we will expel you." (Sira, page 516) This arrangement became an important precedent for Islam's later dealings with non-Muslim tribes and for the future Islamic Empire. Accepting tribute from infidel populations enabled the Muslim state to assimilate non-Muslims without the necessity of converting or killing them. As long as conquered infidel populations were able to pay the jizya (protection tax), they were comparatively safe from Muslim depredations. Of course, as Muhammad stipulated, the Muslims could rescind the agreement at any time.

During the era of the Islamic Empire, subjugated infidel populations became the economic and cultural engines of the Islamic state. The Arab Muslims, nomadic and unlettered, were disposed neither to agriculture, the creation of wealth, nor high culture. The precedent set by Muhammad and his companions was that of raiders and conquerors who were to be served—at the command of God—by other peoples. Without their indigenous populations, the Islamic Empire would have been utterly incapable of maintaining and administrating its vast territories; it could never have developed the impressive infrastructure that it did; and it would never have been mistaken for an advanced, tolerant, cultured civilization by so many modern commentators.

## CONQUEST OF MECCA

Muhammad's greatest victory came in AD 632, ten years after he and his followers had been forced to flee to Medina. In that year, he assembled a force of some ten thousand Muslims and

allied tribes and descended on Mecca. The overawed Meccans immediately sued for peace and received a general amnesty—with some exceptions. Muhammad had no interest in destroying the Meccan population when he could make converts of them and swell the ranks of his armies or exact tribute from them indefinitely. However, he could not abide the continued presence of a few who had in the past ridiculed him and his religion.

> Sira, page 550. The Apostle had instructed his commanders when they entered Mecca only to fight those who resisted them, except a small number who were to be killed even if they were found beneath the curtains of the Kaba.

Among the victims were a former Muslim scribe who had apostatized and the master of two singing girls who had satirized the Apostle.

> Sira, page 551. Another {victim} was al-Huwayyrith bin Nuqaydh bin Wahb bin Abd bin Qusayy, one of those who used to insult him in Mecca.

> Volume 3, Book 29, Number 72. *Narrated Anas bin Malik:* Allah's Apostle entered Mecca in the year of its Conquest wearing an Arabian helmet on his head and when the Prophet took it off, a person came and said, "Ibn Khatal is holding the covering of the Kaba (taking refuge in the Kaba)." The Prophet said, "Kill him."

The conquest of Mecca, though in many ways the high point of Muhammad's career, was in no way the end of his ambitions. With the Meccans vanquished, the Prophet could now turn the energies of the Muslims outward into Yemen (southern and eastern Arabia), north toward Syria, and beyond. But before attacking, Muhammad invited the leaders of the great nations to submit to the will of Allah.

> Volume 4, Book 52, Number 191. *Narrated Abdullah bin Abbas:* In the name of Allah, the most Beneficent, the most Merciful (This letter is) from Muhammad, the slave of Allah, and His Apostle, to Heraclius, the Ruler of the Byzantines. Peace be upon the followers of guidance. Now then, I invite you to Islam (i.e., surrender to Allah), embrace Islam and you will be safe; embrace Islam and Allah will bestow on you a double reward. But if you reject this invitation of Islam, you shall be responsible for misguiding the peasants (i.e., your nation).

Significantly, the Emperor of Ethiopia accepted Muhammad's ultimatum and wrote back swearing fealty. The Byzantine and Persian Emperors, however, laughed his demands out of court. Having failed to accept Islam or Muslim overlordship, the Byzantine and Persian empires thereby rebelled against the will of Allah and would shortly find themselves at war with Islam, whose strength and determination they completely underestimated. Muhammad had great plans for the Muslims:

> Volume 4, Book 52, Number 175. *Narrated Khalid bin Madan:* Um Haram informed us that she heard the Prophet saying, "Paradise is granted to the first batch of my followers who will undertake a naval expedition." Um Haram added, I said, "O Allah's Apostle! Will I be amongst them?" He replied, "You are amongst them." The Prophet then said, "The first army amongst my followers who will invade

Caesar's City will be forgiven their sins." I asked, "Will I be one of them, O Allah's Apostle?" He replied in the negative."

Volume 4, Book 52, Number 177. *Narrated Abu Huraira:* Allah's Apostle said, "The Hour {of the Last Judgment} will not be established until you fight with the Jews, and the stone behind which a Jew will be hiding will say. 'O Muslim! There is a Jew hiding behind me, so kill him.'"

Volume 1, Book 2, Number 24. *Narrated Ibn Umar:* Allah's Apostle said: "I have been ordered (by Allah) to fight against the people until they testify that none has the right to be worshipped but Allah and that Muhammad is Allah's Apostle, and offer the prayers perfectly and give the obligatory charity, so if they perform that, then they save their lives and property from me except for Islamic laws and then their reckoning (accounts) will be done by Allah."

Muhammad died of fever in AD 632, several months after the conquest of Mecca, in the arms of his favorite wife, Aisha, then eighteen years old. He made no explicit provisions for his successor, and after some squabbling, Abu Bakr, Aisha's father, whom Muhammad had designated to lead prayers during his final illness, became the first Caliph. Under Abu Bakr and his three successors—all companions of the Prophet and known as the "four rightly-guided Caliphs"—Islam continued its military expansion and made conquests whose speed and extent are almost without parallel in history.

A great deal of ink has been spilled on the question of Muhammad's moral character. In the concluding chapter of his summary biography, William Montgomery Watt, under the subheading "The Alleged Moral Failures," asks, "How are we to judge Muhammad? By the standards of his own time and country? Or by those of the most enlightened opinion in the West today?"[5] With respect to the former, Watt affirms that Muhammad's "contemporaries did not find him morally defective in any way" and in "both Meccan and Medinan periods Muhammad's contemporaries looked on him as a good and upright man, and in the eyes of history he is a moral and social reformer."[6] Watt, a Scottish Episcopal priest, looks favorably upon Muhammad's personality: "He seems to have been specially fond of children and to have got on well with them . . . He was able to enter into the spirit of childish games and had many friends among children,"[7] and "His kindness extended even to animals, which is remarkable for Muhammad's part of the world."[8]

Watt's sentimentality is typical of modern scholars trying to make up for what they imagine to be centuries of unbalanced criticism of Islam. To describe a man who freely engaged in war, slavery, mass larceny, assassination, massacre, and sexual relations with a child as "a moral and social reformer" who was "fond of children" defies comprehension. But Watt, however befogged his moral reasoning, is really no worse than the countless public personalities today who perform essentially the same act of whitewashing—consciously or unconsciously—whenever they open their mouths about Islam. The consequence of such pathological thinking is to sidetrack meaningful examination of the implications of Muhammad's teachings and example for Muslims and for the lands they inhabit.

Muslims, however, claim that he is a model of conduct and character for all mankind. In so doing they present him for judgment according to the standards of world opinion. Though the world is increasingly becoming one world, it has so far paid scant attention to Muhammad as a moral exemplar.[9]

Indeed, it is high time for the world to realize the danger posed by an ideology that holds up Muhammad as its "moral exemplar." Muhammad, while a man of faith, was decidedly also a man of war. True Muslims throughout history—and today—embrace both aspects of the Prophet. It is a modern prejudice to assume that the two are exclusive. Whatever moderation has found its way into Islam has come from *outside sources*—Christian, classical Greek, Zoroastrian, Hindu, etc. The idea of a moderate Islam is a Western notion that has little meaning within an orthodox Islamic context. Muhammad attests to that. The problem today is that as Islam's presence and power in the West grow, as its institutions and mores gain wider following and acceptance, one may be sure that the deeds of its moral exemplar will follow. With a basic understanding of the sources that govern Muslim behavior, we are now better able to make sense of Islamic history. By examining how Islam expanded since Muhammad and how Muslims through history have sought to follow the example of their Prophet, we will be able to appreciate the danger presented by a resurgent Islam today.

# PART III

# MUHAMMAD'S LEGACY

# 5

# ISLAM UNLEASHED

THE KORAN AND THE SUNNAH ATTEST to the central role violence plays in Islam. Violence is encouraged on the individual level as the only sure means of salvation and enjoined on the collective as a religious duty. As in any religion or ideology, there will always be differing schools of thought and opinion as to how to interpret foundational texts and events. Does Islam permit suicide bombing? The killing of women and children and other non-combatants? Muslims continue to debate these questions and often come up with different answers, which should not be surprising. What is unmistakably clear, however, is that the Koran and the Sunnah lay down an unshakable foundation for organized violence to spread the rule of Sharia for the Muslim faithful. Whatever the social, political, and material factors that have contributed to conflicts between Muslims and non-Muslims throughout history and today, there is something more fundamental than any of them: the violent nature of Islam itself.

Throughout its nearly fourteen-hundred-year history, Islam has waged wars on three continents to spread its political dominion. Islam's military campaigns have at times been swift and spectacularly successful while at other times ponderous and lackluster. Internal squabbles have frequently sapped

Islam's ability to prosecute jihad. When Islam has been able to unite under the banner of one leader (such as the great Saladin, who destroyed the Crusading army in the Holy Land at Hattin in 1187), it has proven itself one of the most formidable military powers in history.

But even when jihad has languished in practice, there has never been any meaningful renunciation of it in principle. Thanks to the eternal and unchanging character of the Koran and the example of Muhammad, making war against non-Muslims is a permanent aspect of the Islamic religion. Expansionary warfare fought in the name of Allah is just as essential to Islam today as it was during the days of Muhammad. While various articulations of Christianity have gone through militarized phases, it is reasonably impossible to derive from the example of Christ and the Apostles a permanent exhortation to commit hostilities against unbelievers. Christian violence is the result of its confusion with non-Christian forces, namely, politics. By contrast, because of Islam's fundamentally political nature, warfare is a consistent and necessary aspect of its expression. The only check to Islam's historical expansion has been its own deficiencies or the superior strength of its enemies. There has been no rejection of Muhammad's policies of military expansion from within Islam, nor could there be without rejecting the very basis of Islam itself: the Koran and the Sunnah.

## THE FIRST WAVE OF JIHAD: THE ARABS

Near the end of his life, Muhammad sent letters to the great empires of the Middle East demanding their submission to his authority. That act dispels any notion that the Prophet intended Islam's expansion to stop at the borders of Arabia. Indeed, it is only logical that, as the fullest and final revelation of Allah to the world, Islam should have universal sway. Thus, as Muhammad had fought and subdued the peoples of the Arabian Peninsula, his successors Abu Bakr, Umar, Uthman, Ali (known as "the four rightly-guided Caliphs"), and others fought and subdued the people of the Middle East, Africa, Asia, and Europe in the name of Allah.

> Volume 4, Book 53, Number 386. *Narrated Jubair bin Haiya: Umar* {the second Caliph} sent the Muslims to the great countries to fight the pagans. . . . When we reached the land of the enemy, the representative of Khosrau {Persia} came out with forty thousand warriors, and an interpreter got up saying, "Let one of you talk to me!" Al-Mughira replied, . . . "Our Prophet, the Messenger of our Lord, has ordered us to fight you till you worship Allah Alone or give Jizya (i.e., tribute); and our Prophet has informed us that our Lord says: "Whoever amongst us is killed (i.e., martyred), shall go to Paradise to lead such a luxurious life as he has never seen, and whoever amongst us remain alive, shall become your master."

Unleashing upon the world the blitzkrieg of its day, Islam rapidly spread into the territories of Byzantium, Persia, and Western Europe in the decades after Muhammad's death (in 632). The creaking Byzantine and Persian powers, having battled each other into mutual decline, offered little resistance to this unanticipated onslaught. The Arab Muslim armies charged into the Holy Land, conquered what is now Iraq and Iran, then swept west across North Africa into Spain and finally into France. The western Muslim offensive was finally halted at the Battle of Poitiers/Tours, not far from Paris, in 732. In the east, the jihad penetrated deep into Central Asia.

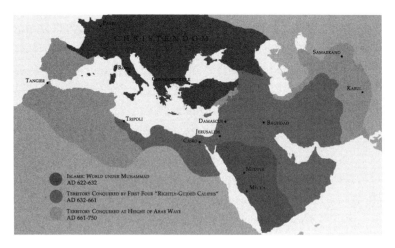

Islamic expansion and control, the Arab Wave. (Map courtesy of author.)

As Muhammad had plundered his foes, so his successors also stripped the conquered areas—incomparably richer both materially and culturally than the desolate sands of Arabia—of their wealth and manpower. Almost overnight, the more advanced civilizations of the Middle East, North Africa, Persia, and Iberia saw their agriculture, native religions, and populations devastated and plundered. Save for a handful of walled cities that managed to negotiate conditional surrenders, the catastrophes those lands suffered were very nearly complete.

Bat Ye'or, a leading scholar of Islam's expansion and treatment of non-Islamic societies, has provided an inestimable service through the compilation and translation of numerous primary source documents describing centuries of Islamic conquest. She includes these documents in her works on Islamic history and the plight of non-Muslims under Islamic rule. They make for disturbing reading. Egypt was one of the first regions to succumb to the Muslim offensive in the seventh century. According to one eyewitness, following the withdrawal of the Byzantine army, "They {the Muslims} seized the town and slaughtered everyone they met in the street and in the churches—men, women, and children, sparing nobody. Then they went to other places, pillaged and killed all the inhabitants they found."[1] In the history of jihad, the slaughter of civilians, the desecration of churches, and the plundering of the country-side are commonplace. Here is Michael the Syrian's account of the Muslim invasion of Cappadocia (southern Turkey) in 650 under Caliph Umar:

> When Muawiya {the Muslim commander} arrived {in Euchaita in Armenia} he ordered all the inhabitants to be put to the sword; he placed guards so that no one escaped. After gathering up all the wealth of the town, they set to torturing the leaders to make them show them things [treasures] that had been hidden. The Taiyaye {Muslim Arabs} led everyone into slavery—men and women, boys and girls—and they committed much debauchery in that unfortunate town: they wickedly committed immoralities inside churches. They returned to their country rejoicing.[2]

Umar, it seems, was a worthy successor to the Prophet. The following description of razzias (raiding expeditions) by the Muslim historian, Ibn al-Athir (1160–1233), in northern Spain and France in the eighth and ninth centuries AD, conveys nothing but satisfaction at the extent of the destruction wrought upon the infidels, including noncombatants.

In 177 [April 17, 793], Hisham, prince of Spain, sent a large army commanded by Abd al-Malik b. Abd al-Wahid b. Mugith into enemy territory, and which made forays as far as Narbonne and Jaranda <Gerona>. This general first attacked Jaranda where there was an elite Frank garrison; he killed the bravest, destroyed the walls and towers of the town and almost managed to seize it. He then marched on to Narbonne, where he repeated the same actions, then, pushing forward, he trampled underfoot the land of the Cerdagne {near Andorra in the Pyrenees}. For several months he traversed this land in every direction, raping women, killing warriors, destroying fortresses, burning and pillaging everything, driving back the enemy who fled in disorder. He returned safe and sound, dragging behind him God alone knows how much booty. This is one of the most famous expeditions of the Muslims in Spain.

In 223 [December 2, 837], Abd ar-Rahman b. al Hakam, sovereign of Spain, sent an army against Alava; it encamped near Hisn al-Gharat, which it besieged; it seized the booty that was found there, killed the inhabitants, and withdrew, carrying off women and children as captives.

In 231 [September 6, 845], a Muslim army advanced into Galicia on the territory of the infidels, where it pillaged and massacred everyone.

In 246 [March 27, 860], Muhammad b. Abd ar-Rahman advanced with many troops and a large military apparatus against the region of Pamplona. He reduced, ruined, and ravaged this territory, where he pillaged and sowed death.[3]

This is hardly the inner struggle that today's Islamic apologists would have us believe that jihad entails. Whereas many religions emphasize some form of spiritual warfare, an interior struggle against an enfeebled or corrupted human nature, Islam emphasizes warfare in the conventional sense. "Raping women, killing warriors, destroying fortresses, burning and pillaging everything" constitute not a war-crimes indictment but a litany of accomplishments and a source of pride.

The above accounts describe just a few events in the first wave of jihad, led by the Arab Muslims that began with the Prophet Muhammad in 622 and concluded a little more than a century later. It is not possible in the limited space here to convey the sheer enormity of the jihad, which amounted to one of the vastest and most destructive military campaigns in world history.

This first wave of jihad engulfed much of the Byzantine, Visigothic, Frankish, and Persian empires and left the newborn Islamic empire controlling territory from southern France, south through Spain, east across North Africa all the way to India, and north to Russia. Early in the second millennium AD, the Mongol invasion from the east greatly weakened the Islamic empire and ended Arab predominance therein. The Mongols, who rivaled the Muslims in the savagery of their conquests, eventually converted to Islam themselves and became the new engines of jihad in the east, a jihad directed largely against Hindu India and Buddhist Indo-China, and which eventually reached the shores of the Pacific.

## THE CRUSADES—IN BRIEF

Islamic rule in the Holy Land began in the second half of the seventh century during the Arab wave of jihad with the conquests of

Damascus and Jerusalem by the second "rightly-guided Caliph," Umar. After the initial bloody campaigns, Christian and Jewish life there was tolerated within the strictures of the dhimma; the Muslim Arabs generally permitted Christians abroad to continue to make pilgrimage to their holy sites, a practice which proved lucrative for the Islamic authorities. In the eleventh century, the relatively benign Arab administration of the Holy Land was replaced with that of Seljuk Turks thanks to their victory in what was effectively a civil war for control of the Islamic empire. Throughout the latter half of the eleventh century, the Turks waged war against the Christian Byzantine empire and pushed it back from its strongholds in Antioch and Anatolia (now Turkey). In 1071, Byzantine forces suffered a crushing defeat at the Battle of Manzikert in what is now Eastern Turkey. The Turks resumed the jihad in the Holy Land, abusing, robbing, enslaving, and killing Christians there and throughout Asia Minor. They threatened to cut off Christendom from its holiest site, the Church of the Holy Sepulchre in Jerusalem, rebuilt under Byzantine stewardship after it was destroyed by Caliph Al-Hakim bi-Amr Allah in 1009.

It was in this context of a renewed jihad in the Middle East that the Roman pope, Urban II, issued a call in 1095 for western Christians to come to the aid of their eastern cousins. This armed pilgrimage, in which numerous civilians as well as soldiers took part, would eventually become known years later as the First Crusade. The idea of a crusade as we now understand that term (as a Christian holy war) developed years later with the rise of such organizations as the Knights Templar that made crusading a way of life. It is worth noting that the most ardent Crusaders, the Franks, were exactly those who had faced jihad and razzias for centuries along the Franco-Spanish border and knew better than most the horrors to which Muslims subjected Christians. At the time of the First Crusade, the populations of Asia Minor, Syria, and Palestine, though ruled by Muslims, were still overwhelmingly Christian. The crusading campaigns of the western Christian armies were justified at the time as a war liberating eastern Christians, whose population, lands, and culture had been devastated by the Turks. Conquering territory for God in the mode of jihad was an alien idea to Christianity, and it should not be surprising that it eventually died out in the west and never gained ascendancy in the east.

I mention the Crusades here because they are so often interpreted oversimplistically as aggressive wars of conquest fought by bloody-minded Christians against peaceful, innocent Muslims. The entry of the Crusaders into Jerusalem in 1099, when they massacred thousands of the inhabitants—Muslims, Jews, and eastern Christians—attests to the savagery of which the Latin armies were capable. There was also the infamous treatment of Jews along the route of the Crusades. These events, however, were resisted and roundly condemned by the Christian authorities—even by the Roman pontiff himself—as gross violations of the principles of a just Christian war. In contrast, centuries of genocidal jihad have never been recognized as outside the letter or spirit of Islam.

Following the capture of Jerusalem in 1099 by the Latin armies and the establishment of the Crusader States in Edessa, Antioch, and Jerusalem, the Muslim and Christian forces fought a see-saw series of wars in which both parties were guilty of the usual gamut of wartime immorality. Over time, even with reinforcing Crusades waged from Europe, the Crusader States, strung out on precarious lines of communication, slowly succumbed to superior Islamic power. In 1271, the last Christian citadel, Antioch, fell to the Muslims. No longer having to divert forces to subdue the Christian beachhead on the eastern Mediterranean, the Muslim armies regrouped for a four-hundred-year-long jihad against southern and eastern Europe, which twice reached as far as Vienna before it was halted. In geostrategic terms, the Crusades can be viewed as an attempt by the West to forestall its own destruction at the hands of Islamic jihad by carrying the fight to the enemy. It worked for a while.

> From the Islamic point of view the crusades were militarily insignificant, mere border raids that were easily beaten back. Emotionally and ideologically, however, they were, and still are, deeply significant. They represent an unforgivable affront, a sacrilege, and the blind intransigence of perverse and stubborn disbelief.[4]

The western Christian guilt still expressed over the Crusades only serves to reinforce the Islamic perception of them as the height of blasphemous insolence on the part of uppity infidels. It is this same dynamic that underlies the persistent violence in the Holy Land to this day. The modern-day Israeli-Palestinian conflict is not merely a question of political resistance by Muslims who refuse to be ruled by non-Muslims; it is a direct result of Allah's command to conquer territory for Islam and to expel the *harbis* (inhabitants of the House of War) from lands once ruled by Islam in the past. This is the explicit teaching of Islam that is echoed throughout the region but that cannot penetrate the circular and illogical reasoning of "leading" Western minds that discard any depiction of Islam as other than a religion of peace.

## THE SECOND WAVE OF JIHAD: THE TURKS

Even as Islam was in the process of being evicted from Spain at the hands of the Roman Catholic armies in the fourteenth and fifteenth centuries (the *Reconquista*), the Muslim Turks waged massive campaigns in Anatolia (Turkey) and the Balkans. One of the most significant resulted in the Battle of Kosovo in 1389, where the Turks, while suffering heavy losses, destroyed a multinational army under the Serbian king St. Lazar. After numerous attempts dating back to the seventh century, Constantinople, the jewel of eastern Christendom, finally fell in 1453 to the armies of Sultan Mahomet II. Lest one ascribe the atrocities of the first wave of jihad to the "Arabness" of its perpetrators, the Turks showed they were fully capable of living up to the principles of the Koran and the Sunnah. Paul Fergosi describes the scene following the final assault on Constantinople:

> Several thousand of the survivors had taken refuge in the cathedral: nobles, servants, ordinary citizens, their wives and children, priests and nuns. They locked the huge doors, prayed, and waited. {Caliph} Mahomet {II} had given the troops free quarter. They raped, of course, the nuns being the first victims, and slaughtered. At least four thousand were killed before Mahomet stopped the massacre at noon. He ordered a *muezzin* {one who issues the call to prayer} to climb into the pulpit of St. Sophia and dedicate the building to Allah. It has remained a mosque ever since. . . . Mahomet asked that the body of the dead emperor be brought to him. Some Turkish soldiers found it in a pile of corpses and recognized Constantine {XI} by the golden eagles embroidered on his boots. The sultan ordered his head to be cut

off and placed between the horse's legs under the equestrian bronze statue of the emperor Justinian. The head was later embalmed and sent around the chief cities of the Ottoman empire for the delectation of the citizens.

Next, Mahomet ordered the Grand Duke Notaras, who had survived, be brought before him, asked him for the names and addresses of all the leading nobles, officials, and citizens, which Notaras gave him. He had them all arrested and decapitated. He sadistically bought from their owners {i.e., Muslim commanders} high-ranking prisoners who had been enslaved, for the pleasure of having them beheaded in front of him.[5]

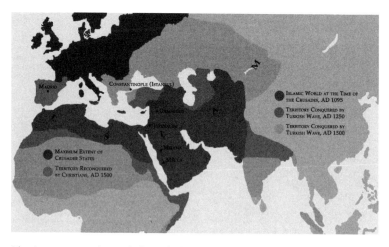

Islamic expansion and control, the Turkish Wave. (Map courtesy of author.)

In one campaign in 1570, the Muslims abrogated a treaty of peace with the Republic of Venice and attacked Cyprus. The citadel of Famagusta held out for nearly a year until Turkish sappers managed to blow up a large part of the defensive wall, which caused the Venetians to come to terms on August 1, 1571. Then, through a ruse, the governor of Famagusta was seized and imprisoned. Fergosi continues:

On August 17, {the Muslim commander} Lala Mustafa ordered {Governor} Bragadino to be taken out of his cell. The time had come for the big show for the people of Famagusta and for his troops. For the Muslim soldiers, it was like a circus day, a moment of relaxation and laughter. For the Christian citizenry of Famagusta the objectives were different, more subtle, more satanic, a moment in the propaganda war, a moment in the war of terror. At the sight of their former Venetian governor, shriven and humiliated, the Cypriots would acquire new respect for their new Turkish masters who had conquered their old Italian masters. By so humiliating the man who had once been the ruler of their daily lives Lala Mustafa wanted to make clear to the citizens of Famagusta that the old order had truly changed. Bragadino was saddled up like a donkey and dragged and kicked around the town like an animal, with bags of dirt and soil tied to his back. Each time he passed before Lala Mustafa he had to lick the ground in front of him. He was then hauled up to the high spar of a galley mast exposed to the multitudes so that all could see what had become of the proud Venetian patrician, now noseless and earless, hauled down and tied to a post. Then Lala Mustafa told him what his fate was to be: to be flayed alive. He died during the torture. His torturers then filled his flayed skin with straw, placed it astride a cow and took this pathetic, tortured effigy, still streaked with blood, around the town under the shelter of a parasol. Then they hung the straw-filled skin, like a large, bloody, bloated balloon, from the yardarm of Lala Mustafa's galley.[6]

This second Turkish wave of jihad reached its farthest extent at the failed sieges of Vienna in 1529 and 1683, where in the latter instance the Muslim army under Kara Mustapha was thrown back by the Roman Catholics under the command of the Polish king, John Sobieski. In the decades that followed, the Ottomans were driven back down through the Balkans, though they were never ejected from the European continent itself. Still, even while the imperial jihad faltered, Muslim land- and sea-borne razzias into Christian territory continued, and Christians were being abducted into slavery from as far away as Ireland into the nineteenth century.

What is striking in the accounts of jihad is not so much the barbaric excesses to which Muslim warriors and rulers have been prone (most societies have been guilty of such crimes at one time or another), but that they follow so naturally from the teachings and example of Muhammad himself. Indeed, excess is an inaccurate term: these deeds of savagery are only excessive when viewed from a non-Islamic perspective. They are perfectly in line with Islamic instructions to conquer, kill, pillage, and humiliate the infidel as enjoined in the Koran and exemplified by the life of Muhammad. The barbarous end to Bragadino, for example, is not so far from that of Kinana bin al-Rabi, whom the Prophet ordered burned and beheaded. The regular massacres of civilians and the enslavement of women and children that punctuate Islam's history all have precedent in Muhammad's campaigns. Whereas, say, Christian barbarism identifiably contradicts the teachings and example of Christ,

Islamic barbarism stems directly from the Muslims' basic statement of faith that "there is no God but Allah and Muhammad is his Prophet."

# 6

# THE DHIMMI

ISLAM'S PERSECUTION OF NON-MUSLIMS IS IN no way limited to jihad, even though that is the basic relationship between the Muslim and non-Muslim world. After the jihad concludes in a given area with the conquest of infidel territory, the dhimma (treaty of protection), may be granted to the conquered People of the Book—historically, Jews, Christians, and Zoroastrians. The dhimma provides that the life and property of the infidel are exempted from jihad for as long as the Muslim rulers permit, which has generally meant for as long as the subject non-Muslims—the dhimmi—prove economically useful to the Islamic state. The Koran spells out the payment of the jizya (poll- or head-tax; Sura 9:29), which is the most conspicuous means by which the Muslim overlords exploit the dhimmi. But the jizya is not merely economic in its function; it exists also to humiliate the dhimmi and impress on him the superiority of Islam. Al-Maghili, a fifteenth century Muslim theologian, explains:

> On the day of payment {of the jizya} they {the dhimmis} shall be assembled in a public place like the *suq* {place of commerce}. They should be standing there waiting in the lowest and dirtiest place. The acting officials representing the

Law shall be placed above them and shall adopt a threatening attitude so that it seems to them, as well as to others, that our object is to degrade them by pretending to take their possessions. They will realize that we are doing them a favor <again> in accepting from them the jizya and letting them <thus> go free.[1]

In his discussion of the jizya, Al-Maghili affirms the underlying principle that "might belongs to Allah, his Prophet, and to the believers," which sums up the Islamic view of justice quite neatly. The Western understanding of justice sees it as independent of power, and indeed, very often the victim of power; the fate of just men such as Christ and Socrates attests to this. Christ and Socrates are just men because they proclaim truth and are willing to perish rather than relinquish it. Muhammad, on the other hand, is a just man in the Islamic tradition because he was a vehicle for truth—the word of Allah—*and* because he triumphed over his enemies—had he failed in his campaigns, his religious message never would have succeeded.

The Islamic concept of martyrdom further conflates might and right. Whereas a Christian martyr *dies* for his faith, a Muslim martyr first *kills* for it; dying for the truth makes no sense in an Islamic context if the enemy remains unharmed. Christ instructs that blessed are the poor, the meek, the wrongly persecuted; Islam teaches that blessed are they who use power to make the law of Allah dominant over others. A Muslim martyr is known by the term *shahid*, meaning "witness." A shahid witnesses or testifies to the truth of Islam by "killing and being killed" (Sura 9:111).

Islamic law codifies various other restrictions on the dhimmi, all of which derive from the Koran and the Sunnah. Several hundred years of Islamic thought on the right treatment of dhimmi peoples is summed up by Al-Damanhuri, a seventeenth-century head of Al-Azhar University in Cairo, the most prestigious center for learning in the Muslim world:

> Just as the dhimmis are prohibited from building churches, other things also are prohibited to them. They must not assist an unbeliever against a Muslim . . . raise the cross in an Islamic assemblage . . . display banners on their own holidays; bear arms . . . or keep them in their homes. Should they do anything of the sort, they must be punished, and the arms seized. . . . The Companions [of the Prophet] agreed upon these points in order to demonstrate the abasement of the infidel and to protect the weak believer's faith. For if he sees them humbled, he will not be inclined toward their belief, which is not true if he sees them in power, pride, or luxury garb, as all this urges him to esteem them and incline toward them, in view of his own distress and poverty. Yet esteem for the unbeliever is unbelief.[2]

This discussion further illustrates the Islamic confusion of might and right. "Faith" follows from the demonstrable superiority of Islamic institutions over those of other religions. Permitting, say, a great cathedral in Islamic territory risks the impression that the Christian God is greater than the Islamic one.

In Islam, "peace" implies the rule of Sharia law and "tolerance" the dhimma. The dhimmi's Muslim masters tolerate them to live and procreate, to prosper and forfeit their wealth to the Islamic state, and even to worship in a limited fashion. But this tolerance is certainly not based in anything like a Western conception of natural or civil rights; moreover, the modest rights granted by the dhimma are unilaterally revocable. The jizya amounts to protection money paid to the Islamic state to safeguard life and limb. If one cannot pay, one's life and property become forfeit. It is worth mentioning here that if one is not a person "of the Book" but is, say, a pagan or an atheist, the option of the dhimma is not available: one must choose between conversion to Islam and death.

The Christian, Jewish, and Zoroastrian peoples of the Middle East, North Africa, and much of Europe suffered under the oppressive strictures of the dhimma for centuries. The status of these dhimmi peoples is comparable in many ways to that of former slaves in the post-bellum American South. Forbidden to construct houses of worship or repair extant ones, economically crippled by the jizya, socially humiliated, legally discriminated against, and generally kept in a permanent state of weakness and vulnerability by the Muslim overlords, it should not be surprising that their numbers dwindled, in some places to the point of extinction. The once large Christian and Jewish populations of Iraq, Syria, Turkey, and North Africa have been virtually wiped out. One of the largest indigenous groups still left in the Islamic world, the Coptic Christians of Egypt, suffer routine discrimination and persecution, which frequently flares into open violence and terrorism.

Hindus, whom Muslims considered pagans for centuries, suffered what may amount to the greatest genocide in world history, known in the East as "The Hindu Holocaust." This was a series of invasions into South Asia, first by Arab armies and later by Turks and Mongols, which killed incalculable millions. "The massacres perpetrated by Muslims in India are unparalleled in history, bigger in sheer numbers than the {Nazi}

Holocaust, or the massacre of the Armenians by the Turks; more extensive even than the slaughter of the South American native populations by the invading Spanish and Portuguese."[3] This lengthy history of Islamic aggression and massacre served as the foundation for the twentieth century Wars of Partition fought between Islamic Pakistan and Bangladesh and Hindu India. The Muslim-Hindu conflict simmers to this day in the ongoing dispute over the province of Kashmir and in the form of sporadic Muslim terrorism in the region. The bombing of a train in Mumbai (Bombay) in July 2006, which killed more than two hundred, is but a relatively recent episode in the millennium-long Islamic-Hindu conflict.

Should the dhimmi violate the conditions of the dhimma—perhaps through practicing his own religion indiscreetly or failing to show adequate deference to a Muslim—then the jihad resumes. At various times in Islamic history, dhimmi peoples rose above their subjected status, and this was often the occasion for violent reprisals by Muslim populations who believed them to have violated the terms of the dhimma. Medieval Andalusia (Moorish Spain) is often pointed out by Muslim apologists as a kind of multicultural wonderland in which Jews and Christians were permitted by the Islamic government to rise through the ranks of learning and government administration. What we are not told, however, is that this relaxation of the disabilities resulted in widespread rioting on the part of the Muslim populace that killed hundreds of dhimmis, mainly Jews. By refusing to convert to Islam and straying from the traditional constraints of the dhimma (even at the behest of the Islamic government, which was in need of capable manpower), the dhimmi had implicitly chosen the only other option permitted by Sharia law: death.

## THE HOUSE OF WAR

When analyzing the history of jihad and dhimmitude, it is imperative to keep in mind that both are based directly on the Koran and the Sunnah. While Muslims will surely disagree about the rightness and efficacy of specific policies at any given time, what they are invariably trying to determine (insofar as they are good Muslims) is what the Koran and the Sunnah dictate in a given instance: "What would Muhammad do?"—a question that will often lead to a very different answer than, say, "What would Jesus do?"

Due to the political nature of Islam—or, more precisely, due to its total lack of differentiation between the political and the religious—the question of "What would Muhammad do?" applies as much to one's military strategy, international diplomacy, and social policy as to how one should pray or wash one's hands. Islam is, in a word, totalitarian.

Jihad and dhimmitude—the two orthodox ways that Muslims are to deal with non-Muslims—and their attendant practical requirements originate from within Islam itself—they are explicit commands from Allah—and are not the product of outside historical forces in the way that the idea of holy war in Western Christendom took centuries to develop and then faded away. The institutions of jihad and dhimmitude are divinely enjoined and are therefore non-negotiable. Ibn Abi Zayd al-Qayrawani (922-96), one of the most influential Muslim jurisprudents of Islam's first centuries, makes it clear:

> Jihad is a precept of divine institution. Its performance by certain individuals may dispense others from it. We Malikis [one of the four schools of Muslim jurisprudence] maintain

that it is preferable not to begin hostilities with the enemy before having invited the latter to embrace the religion of Allah except where the enemy attacks first. They have the alternative of either converting to Islam or paying the poll tax [jizya], short of which war will be declared against them.

It is incumbent upon us to fight the enemy without inquiring as to whether we shall be under the command of a pious or depraved leader.[4]

The principal schools of Islamic jurisprudence, while differing somewhat in their interpretation of Sharia law, are in total agreement on the necessity of the Umma to conquer the world for Allah. While there is some disagreement on ancillary questions such as how the infidel should be treated after conquest, how the war should be conducted, the circumstances under which women and children may be considered combatants, etc., there is no doubt anywhere about the basic rightness and necessity of jihad. The Muslim historian Ibn Khaldun (1332–1406) succinctly sums up the doctrine of jihad and the distinctions between Islamic and non-Islamic principles of governance:

In the Muslim community, the holy war is a religious duty, because of the universalism of the [Muslim] mission and [the obligation to] convert everybody to Islam either by persuasion or by force. Therefore, caliphate and royal authority are united [in Islam], so that the person in charge can devote the available strength to both of them [religion and politics] at the same time.

The other religious groups did not have a universal mission, and the holy war was not a religious duty to them, save only for purposes of defence. . . . It {royal authority} comes to them as the necessary result of group feeling, which by its very nature seeks to obtain royal authority, as we have mentioned before, and not because they are under obligation to gain power over other nations, as is the case with Islam. They are merely required to establish their religion among their own [people] . . .

There were dissensions among the Christians with regard to their religion and to Christology. . . . [To] discuss or argue those things with them is not up to us. It is [for them to choose between] conversion to Islam, payment of the poll tax, or death.[5]

And just as jihad has remained intrinsic to Islam in the modern era, so has Islamic scholarship on the imperative of jihad remained central to Islamic thinking. Take, for instance, this tract by Hassan Al-Banna, the founder of the Muslim Brotherhood, which is today one of the most influential organizations in Egypt:

Jihad is an obligation from Allah on every Muslim and cannot be ignored nor evaded. Allah has ascribed great importance to jihad and has made the reward of the martyrs and the fighters in His way a splendid one. Only those who have acted similarly and who have modeled themselves upon the martyrs in their performance of jihad can join them in this reward. Furthermore, Allah has specifically honoured the *Mujahideen* {jihadists} with certain exceptional qualities, both spiritual and practical, to benefit them in this world and the next. Their pure blood is a symbol of victory in this world and the mark of success and felicity in the world to come.

Many Muslims today mistakenly believe that fighting the enemy is *jihad asghar* (a lesser jihad) and that fighting one's ego is *jihad akbar* (a greater jihad). The following narration [*athar*] is quoted as proof: "'We have returned from the lesser jihad to embark on the greater jihad.' They said: 'What is the greater jihad?' He {the Prophet Muhammad} said: 'The jihad of the heart, or the jihad against one's ego.'"

This narration is used by some to lessen the importance of fighting, to discourage any preparation for combat, and to deter any offering of jihad in Allah's way. This narration is not a saheeh (sound) tradition.

Nevertheless, even if it were a sound tradition, it would never warrant abandoning jihad or preparing for it in order to rescue the territories of the Muslims and repel the attacks of the disbelievers.[6]

While the fact that Islam sees no separation between religion and government is often pointed out, its logical implications rarely seem to be appreciated. A system of government in which the state power is employed to enforce religious doctrine is, of course, a theocracy. It is astonishing that so many Westerners can become greatly exercised over questions of the separation of church and state in their own societies and yet fail to appreciate the implications of a system of belief that ostensibly rejects such a separation in principle. A brief glance at Saudi Arabia, for example, a nation that has remained faithful to the precepts of Sharia, should be enough to establish to any Westerner Islam's totalitarian characteristics. There is no distinction between rendering unto Caesar and to God in Islam because Allah is Caesar and has given the world the model for the just and holy society in the Koran and the Sunnah.

Muhammad's life and teachings not only delineate the over-arching strategic aim of Islam—continuous political-military expansion—but they shed invaluable light on the proper means by which that conquest is to take place. Open warfare is the most obvious tactic Islam has at its disposal, but Muhammad also demonstrated himself a man of subtlety and patience when it came to dealing with a stronger foe—as have his successors. We have seen that he freely employed assassination to rid himself of detractors. Really, no stratagem may be considered outside Islam's accepted arsenal inasmuch as it considers itself in a permanent state of war with the non-Muslim world. Terrorism is a means to an end; the end is Islamic hegemony over the earth. Thus, defeating terrorism will not solve the problem—in such a case, Islam will merely assume a different tactic, whatever that might be.

It is not hard to see that the only proper way to regard Islam is not as a religion at all. Thanks to the legacy of Christianity, Westerners instinctively regard religion as a personal issue that is naturally distinct from the political realm. What they fail to bear in mind, however, is that Western political traditions grew out of the experience of Christianity with its emphasis on the division between God and Caesar. It is folly to believe that a Western political model can pacify Islam's violent ways precisely because such a model presupposes a Christian heritage. Islam is much more aptly regarded as a political ideology more akin to National Socialism and Communism than any religion familiar to a Westerner.

## THE HOUSE OF LIES

And, unfortunately, we must not rely on Muslims themselves to tell us these worrisome truths. Due to the state of war between the House of Islam and the House of War, lying to the enemy infidel is an acceptable tactic. The parroting by Muslim organizations today throughout dar al-harb that Islam is a religion of peace or that the origins of Islamic violence lie in the unbalanced psyches of particular individual fanatics must be considered as disinformation intended to induce the infidel world to let down its guard. Of course, individual Muslims may genuinely regard their religion as peaceful but only due to ignorance. A telling point is that, while Muslims who present their religion as peaceful abound throughout dar al-harb, they are nearly non-existent in dar al-Islam. A Muslim apostate once suggested to me a litmus test for Westerners who believe that Islam is a religion of peace and tolerance: try making that point on a street corner in Ramallah, or Riyadh, or Islamabad, or anywhere in the Muslim world. He assured me that you would not live five minutes. We are being dealt a pack of lies.

> {A} problem concerning law and order {with respect to Muslims in dar al-harb} arises from an ancient Islamic legal principle—that of *taqiyya*, a word the root meaning of which is "to remain faithful" but which in effect means "dissimulation". It has full Koranic authority (92:17 and 49:13) and allows the Muslim to conform outwardly to the requirements of unislamic or non-Islamic government, while inwardly "remaining faithful" to whatever he conceives to be proper Islam, while waiting for the tide to turn.[7]

> Volume 4, Book 52, Number 269. *Narrated Jabir bin Abdullah:* The Prophet said, "War is deceit."

Examples of taqiyya include permission to renounce Islam itself in order to save one's neck or ingratiate oneself with an enemy. It is not hard to see that the implications of taqiyya are insidious in the extreme: they essentially render negotiated settlement—and, indeed, all veracious communication between Muslims and non-Muslims—suspect. It should not, however, be surprising that a party to a war should seek to mislead the other about its means and intentions.

> "Taqiyya" is the religiously-sanctioned doctrine, with its origins in Shia Islam but now practiced by non-Shia as well, of deliberate dissimulation about religious matters that may be undertaken to protect Islam, and the Believers. A related term, of broader application, is "kitman," which is defined as "mental reservation." An example of "Taqiyya" would be the insistence of a Muslim apologist that "of course" there is freedom of conscience in Islam, and then quoting that Qur'anic verse—"There shall be no compulsion in religion." {2:256} But the impression given will be false, for there has been no mention of the Muslim doctrine of abrogation, or naskh, whereby such an early verse as that about "no compulsion in religion" has been cancelled out by later, far more intolerant and malevolent verses. In any case, history shows that within Islam there is, and always has been, "compulsion in religion" for Muslims, and for non-Muslims. . . .

> "Kitman" is close to "taqiyya," but rather than outright dissimulation, it consists in telling only a part of the truth, with "mental reservation" justifying the omission of the rest. One example may suffice. When a Muslim maintains that "jihad" really means "a spiritual struggle," and fails to add that this

definition is a recent one in Islam (little more than a century old), he misleads by holding back, and is practicing "kitman." When he adduces, in support of this doubtful proposition, the hadith in which Muhammad, returning home from one of his many battles, is reported to have said... that he had returned from "the Lesser Jihad to the Greater Jihad" and does not add what he also knows to be true, that this is a "weak" hadith, regarded by the most respected muhaddithin as of doubtful authenticity, he is further practicing "kitman."[8]

In times when the greater strength of dar al-harb necessitates that the jihad take an indirect approach, the natural attitude of a Muslim to the infidel world must be one of deception and omission. Revealing frankly the ultimate goal of dar al-Islam to conquer and plunder dar al-harb when the latter holds the military trump cards would be strategic idiocy. Fortunately for the jihadists, most non-Muslims do not understand how one is to read the Koran, nor do they trouble themselves to find out what Muhammad actually did and taught, which makes it easy to give the impression through selective quotations and omissions that Islam is a religion of peace. Any infidel who wants to believe such fiction will happily persist in his mistake, having been cited a handful of Meccan verses and being told that Muhammad was a man of great piety and charity. The Islamic world knows better, and it is about time that we did.

> A people that is not prepared to kill and to die in order to create a just society cannot expect any support from Allah. The Almighty has promised us that the day will come when the whole of mankind will live united under the banner of Islam, when the sign of the Crescent, the symbol of

Muhammad, will be supreme everywhere.... But that day must be hastened through our Jihad, through our readiness to offer our lives and to shed the unclean blood of those who do not see the light brought from the Heavens by Muhammad in his *miraj* {'nocturnal voyages to the "court" of Allah'}. . . . It is Allah who puts the gun in our hand. But we cannot expect Him to pull the trigger as well simply because we are faint-hearted.[9]

# 7

# JIHAD IN THE MODERN ERA

IT MAY BE TEMPTING TO REGARD Islam's violent persecution of infidels as an anachronism that no longer operates in modern times. But the absence of large-scale jihad in the modern era is due not to a change within Islam but to the changing balance of forces between the House of Islam and the House of War. Following the defeat of the Muslim armies outside Vienna in the late seventeenth century, the Islamic empire began a steep decline and lost the wherewithal to threaten non-Muslim lands. In the modern era, jihad has been focused mainly on dhimmis living within the House of Islam and, in the past several decades, to acts of terrorism and guerilla warfare against the House of War.

## THE ARMENIAN GENOCIDE

In the nineteenth century, pressure from the more powerful Western nations—principally Great Britain—compelled the Muslim Ottoman Empire (later Turkey) to grant greater rights to its dhimmi populations. In 1856, the dhimma was formally suspended in the empire, thus freeing dhimmi peoples from their many disabilities—though also withdrawing the protection the dhimma granted them from the Muslim population. The social and economic ascendancy of former dhimmi peoples in Ottoman lands soon became the occasion for brutal reprisals. The late nineteenth century witnessed the first wave of the Armenian genocide in which hundreds of thousands of Armenian Christians were ejected from their homes, deported, assaulted, marched into the wilderness to die, or simply slain on the spot. Waves of genocidal jihad against the Armenians continued throughout the closing years of the nineteenth century and into the twentieth, sometimes with the active involvement of the Ottoman government or sometimes with its tacit permission.

The opening act of the Armenian genocide followed the Turkish massacre of thirty thousand Bulgarians in 1876, which had resulted in the Russo-Turkish War, the Congress of Berlin, and Bulgarian independence. The Armenian genocide illustrates the fact that even in the modern era jihad is still an operative (if sometimes latent) principle within the Umma.

While the massacres of the Armenians, like any significant historical event, were bound up with various political, economic, and other factors, they were also unmistakably religious in nature. Thanks to numerous foreign eyewitnesses, the events of the genocide (1896–1923) are well documented. Peter Balakian's book, *The Burning Tigris*, conveys the horrific story. One special point of relevance to our discussion is that Muslim clerics and theological students, who knew the Koran and the Sunnah better than most, often led the massacres and "seemed essentially and continually motivated to kill {Armenian} Christians."[1] The British consul, Henry Barnham, described the carnage that he witnessed in Aleppo Province in Armenian Turkey in 1896:

> The butchers and tanners, with sleeves tucked up to the
> shoulders, armed with clubs and cleavers, cut down the

Christians, with cries of "Allahu Akbar!" {God is great!} broke down the doors of the houses with pickaxes and levers, or scaled the walls with ladders. Then when mid-day came they knelt down and said their prayers, and then jumped up and resumed the dreadful work, carrying it on far into the night. Whenever they were unable to break down the doors they fired the houses with petroleum . . . [2]

The Islamic religious leaders would rally the mob by chanting prayers, and mosques were often used as places to gather bloodthirsty crowds. Throughout the land, Christians were murdered in the name of Allah. One survivor recounted the destruction of two churches in the town of Severek in the province of Diyarbekir:

The mob had plundered the Gregorian church, desecrated it, murdered all who had sought shelter there, and, as a sacrifice, beheaded the sexton on the stone threshold. Now it filled our yard. The blows of an axe crashed in the church doors. The attackers rushed in, tore the Bibles and hymnbooks to pieces, broke and shattered whatever they could, blasphemed the cross and, as a sign of victory, chanted the Mohammedan prayer: "La ilaha ill-Allah, Muhammedin Rasula-llah" (There is no God but one God, and Mohammed is His prophet) . . . The leader of the mob cried: "Muhammede salavat!" Believe in Mohammed and deny your religion. No one answered. . . . The leader gave the order to massacre. The first attack was on our pastor. The blow of an axe decapitated him. His blood, spurting in all directions, spattered the walls and ceiling.[3]

A Turkish soldier in Erzurum recounted the massacres to his to his family in two letters that eventually came into the hands of a British consul.

> My brother, if you want news from here we have killed 1,200 Armenians, all of them food for the dogs. . . . Mother, I am safe and sound. Father, 20 days ago we made war on the Armenian unbelievers. Through God's grace no harm befell us. There is a rumor afoot that our Battalion will be ordered to your part of the world—if so, we will kill all the Armenians there. Besides, 511 Armenians were wounded, one or two perish every day. If you ask after the soldiers and Bashi Bazouks, not one of their noses has bled. . . . May God bless you.
>
> The next morning {December 29, 1896} the Turkish troops fired through the church windows {in Urfa—ancient Edessa—where many had taken refuge from the slaughter} and broke down the iron door, mockingly calling on "Christ now to prove himself a greater prophet than Mohammed." They began killing everyone on the floor of the church by hand or with pistols. From the altar they gunned down the women and children in the gallery. Finally the Turks gathered bedding and straw, on which "they poured some thirty cans of kerosene" and set the church ablaze.[4]

The massacres often began as acts of mob violence by Muslim civilians egged on by religious and secular authorities. When outraged foreign witnesses complained to the Turkish government, soldiers were sent in, ostensibly to restore order, but who invariably abetted the violence with more efficient instruments.[5] Apart from the rare escape, the pitiful few who survived did so through the only ways permitted to them by the Koran: they converted to Islam or were taken as *fay* (booty) by the jihadists, i.e., slaves. Numerous Armenian women were forced into harems. The jihad against the Armenians in the 1890s, while it claimed a staggering 250,000 lives, only prefigured the wholesale genocide set in motion in 1915. The 1915 massacres would prove to be the first "modern" genocide in which a state's full military and industrial apparatus would be employed for the mass murder of unarmed civilians. The isolation and imprisonment of the target group's cultural leaders, the separation of able-bodied men from women and children through conscription into "labor battalions," and the confiscation of arms are by now familiar tactics. Yet while the means were often modern, the central motivation was hardly new.

> To promote the idea of jihad, the sheikh-ul-Islam's {the most senior religious leader in the Ottoman Empire} published proclamation summoned the Muslim world to arise and massacre its Christian oppressors. "Oh Moslems," the document read, "Ye who are smitten with happiness and are on the verge of sacrificing your life and your good for the cause of right, and of braving perils, gather now around the Imperial throne." In the Ikdam, the Turkish newspaper that had just passed into German ownership, the idea of jihad was underscored: "The deeds of our enemies have brought down the wrath of God. A gleam of hope has appeared. All Mohammedans, young and old, men, women, and children must fulfill their duty. . . . If we do it, the deliverance of the subjected Mohammedan kingdoms is assured." . . . "He who kills even one unbeliever," one pamphlet read, "of those who rule over us, whether he does it secretly or openly, shall be rewarded by God."[6]

Even while the 1915 genocide soon took on an industrial scale, the killing also proceeded at a more grass-roots level. Mobs of Muslim civilians armed with axes, swords, pikes, and other primitive weapons, whipped into a religious frenzy, would roam Armenian quarters looking for victims. Leslie Davis, American consul in Harput, tried to save as many Armenians as possible by hiding them in the large consulate building during the summer of 1915. Soon he had to put them in the consulate garden for lack of room.

> The garden was large, with high walls and mulberry trees that provided good cover for the refugees. All that summer about forty Armenians slept outside in that garden. And each night everyone at the consulate could hear the Turks in the square in front of the building holding prayer meetings. "We could all hear them piously calling upon Allah to bless them in their efforts to kill the hated Christians," Davis recorded. "Night after night this same chant went up to heaven and day after day these Turks carried on their bloody work."[7]

In a candid moment, a Muslim Turkish captain explained to an Armenian priest the holy nature of the genocide.

> When the Armenian priest continued by asking him how he would "atone for his sins" in the "other world," the captain answered: "I have already atoned for them as I've always done after such killings. . . . I spread out my prayer rug and pray, giving glory to Allah and the Prophet who made me worthy of personally participating in the holy jihad in these days of my old age."[8]

As the Koran and the Sunnah teach, killing in jihad is not a sin to be atoned for but a blessing and a virtue for which the pious Muslim owes thanks to Allah. The captain told the priest that his district governor, Mehmed Kemal, had "made a vow on the honor of the prophet: I shall not leave a single Armenian alive in the *sanjak*{district} of Yozgat" (Balakian 338). Kemal was good to his word: sixty thousand men, women, children, and infants were massacred, some 90 percent of the population, in his province alone.[9] Throughout Turkey in 1915, 1.5 million perished.

In 1922, the last act of this horrible ordeal took place at Smyrna on the Mediterranean coast. Here the inhabitants—Christian Armenians and Greeks—were surrounded by the Turkish army and systematically massacred. Few lived to tell the tale. To complete the work, the Turks burnt the historic city to the ground. And to their eternal shame, Allied British, French, and American warships anchored at Smyrna maintained an attitude of non-interference. Indeed, the Allied commanders ordered their bands to play at full volume to drown out the death agonies of those ashore and turned water cannon on swimmers trying to climb their vessels' anchor chains. More than 150,000 died in five days of butchery. From 1915–23, some 2.5 million Greek and Armenian Christians perished at the hands of Muslim Turks. Having begun the twentieth century with some 4.5 million Christian inhabitants, Turkey now possesses perhaps a hundred thousand. Though shocking, such episodes of barbarism are hardly worse than what occurs to this day to non-Muslims in the ongoing conflicts in the Sudan, Nigeria, Indonesia, Iraq, Syria, the Philippines, etc. at the hands of dutiful jihadists.

If the Armenian genocide sounds familiar, that's because it is: the methods, scale, and sheer fastidiousness by which it was carried out prefigure the Nazi genocide almost to the letter. Indeed, numerous German statesmen and military personnel were in Turkey (their World War I ally) at the time, and it certainly seems that they learned a thing or two. The Armenian genocide set the terrible precedent that it was possible for a modern government to murder huge numbers of people and basically get away with it. On the eve of unleashing his genocidal war machine on Europe, Adolf Hitler reassured his subordinates, "Who, after all, remembers the Armenians?" Even though the atrocities against Armenians were extensively documented by foreign eyewitnesses and widely broadcast by the international media (and even admitted to by many of the perpetrators), few today seem to be aware of them. The persistent Western ignorance of the Armenian genocide mirrors Western ignorance of the nature of Islam.

To this day, the Turkish government denies the genocide and insists that any deaths resulted from insurrection on the part of the Armenians—a lie equivalent to blaming European Jews for their mass murder in the 1940s or Russian Christians for their slaughter at the hands of the Soviet government. All too often, Westerners have acquiesced in the Turks' cover-up lest they offend a strategic partner. Even today, Turkey remains in negotiations to enter the European Union without having acknowledged—let alone atoned for—her past crimes.

## POST-IMPERIAL JIHAD

With the breakup of the Ottoman Empire and the end of the Caliphate following World War I, the Umma lost its symbolic unity. The newly created Muslim nations found themselves outclassed by the far more advanced Western powers. Britain and France carved up the old Empire between them and ultimately created from it the nation-states of the Middle East of today. The period between the World Wars was the nadir of the Islamic world when large portions of the House of Islam were occupied and directly administered by infidels.

The collapse of the Ottoman Empire was a manifest disaster for Islam, but since World War II the situation has been improving. With the decline of European colonialism and the preoccupation of the two superpowers with each other during the Cold War, the House of Islam gained a new lease on life. With the nettling exception of Israel (and to a lesser degree, Spain), the post–World War II process of decolonization restored Muslim lands to Muslim rule. The decline of the Western European powers provided assurance that the House of War was on the wane and that the future would see the return of the Umma to its rightful, Allah-ordained place in the sun. The major conflicts of the twentieth century were not between the House of Islam and the House of War but among the non-Muslim nations themselves, which served to reinforce the Koranic description of the quarrelsome, bellicose infidel nations who refuse to submit to the divinely prescribed order of things. The dependence of the House of War on oil and the fact that Muslim states control so much of it is viewed as yet another gift from Allah, who was once again preparing his people for greatness.

Following post–World War II decolonization, the most obvious target for jihad was the newly created state of Israel, which committed the unpardonable affront of claiming Islamic land for infidels. While the Muslim states have so far proven unable to rid themselves of the Jewish state through open warfare, they have, over time, been able to make headway through a combination of negotiation and support for terrorism. By way of terrorist groups such as Hamas and Hezbollah, the Islamic nations have been able to fight a proxy war against Israel while minimizing danger to themselves. Those caught in the middle are the Israeli and Palestinian citizenry, who must endure varying levels of terrorism, oppression, and conflict. The dwindling number of Christians in the region, with virtually no representation, have perhaps suffered the most.

But Israel has hardly been the only target of jihad in recent years. Over the past few decades, organized Muslim violence against infidels has occurred throughout North Africa, the Balkans, Iraq, the Caucusus, Indonesia, Western China, Kashmir, etc. Hundreds of thousands—likely millions—have died in the Sudanese civil wars over the past forty years. Those wars were complex, but they were essentially a jihad fought by Arab Muslims against black Christians and animists. The most spectacularly successful jihad in recent memory was that carried out in Afghanistan against the Soviet Union from 1979–89. In Afghanistan, jihadists such as Osama bin Laden honed their skills and demonstrated their worthiness as holy fighters in the way of Allah. While the West tends to view the Soviets' abandonment of Afghanistan and the collapse of the Soviet Bloc in 1991 as its own victory over Communism, it was similarly interpreted by the Muslim world as a victory for Islam over an infidel superpower. It is probably difficult to overestimate the tonic power that throwing the Soviets out of Afghanistan lent to the global Islamic revival.

The success in Afghanistan coupled with the toppling ten years before of a United States client government, the Iranian Shah, by a popular Islamic revolution, lent momentum to what appeared to be an Islamic comeback. The 1990s brought further victories: the humiliation of the United States in Somalia by Muslim paramilitaries; the successful bid for statehood by Muslim-led Bosnia (with Western help); the successful expulsion of Christian Serbs from Kosovo by Albanian jihadists (again, with Western help); the lack of a total American victory against Saddam Hussein in the first Gulf War; and the successful terrorist attacks on US interests in Africa and the Middle East (the Nairobi Embassy, USS Cole, etc.). The crowning achievement, of course, was the spectacular strikes on the American homeland in 2001. While there is no apparent central command that orchestrates the disparate states, organizations, and individuals that wage jihad around the world, they nonetheless share a common motivation and strategic goal as set out in the Koran and the Sunnah.

Since the attacks of September 11, 2001, Islamic jihad has experienced some reverses at the hands of superior Western (mainly American) firepower. The Taliban, a strict Sharia regime, was handily thrown out of Afghanistan in 2001 by the US-led coalition. Similarly, the Iraqi army crumpled in the face of the American offensive in the spring of 2003. But it remains obvious that the initial victories in those countries are hardly the end of the story. In Iraq, the American-backed Shia government alienated its large Sunni minority, which in turn opened it up to the rise of the terrorist "Islamic State" in northern Iraq and Syria, which threatens to rend Iraq asunder. Both regimes in Iraq and Afghanistan, while nominally democratic, have adopted major elements of Sharia law. What the outcome of the enterprises in Afghanistan and Iraq will prove to be, time alone will tell. We can, however, say with confidence that as long as Islam remains a potent force in those countries as elsewhere, violence and tyranny will prove more the norm than the exception.

# PART IV

# THE DANGER NOW

# 8

# THE ELEPHANT IN THE ROOM

AT VARIOUS TIMES IN HISTORY THERE has been an elephant in the room on the world stage: something so obvious and yet so disquieting that most people refuse to see it for what it is. At such times, even the best educated and most informed take refuge in socially acceptable platitudes and vagaries that asphyxiate serious analysis and prevent remedial action. In the 1930s, the elephant in the room was a revanchist Germany. In light of the catastrophe of World War I, the idea that any nation could be preparing for a new war was so terrible that it proved psychologically unacceptable; many people simply would not believe it, no matter how striking the evidence. It is almost unbelievable today to reflect on how the elites of Europe in the 1930s failed to recognize where events were leading. German foreign policy was increasingly belligerent in the midst of a crash rearmament program, and the Nazi hierarchy consistently and publicly expressed its revanchist goals. That Germany's leaders were outlining a plan for European conquest and the destruction of "undesirable" races, however, was simply too awful to accept—and so it wasn't. After the disasters of World War II and its accompanying genocide, the free nations pledged "never again"—never would they let such a destructive regime gain ascendancy on the world stage. Of course, in just a few years' time, another militarized ideology, Communism, had crushed freedom in Eastern Europe, conquered China, blockaded Berlin, and invaded South Korea. The Nazi genocide, far from being the last, turned out to be one of many, inspired mostly by Communism in Eastern Europe, Asia, and Africa that altogether claimed an almost unimaginable 100 million lives in the twentieth century.[1] The Munich Agreement of September 1938 by which Great Britain and France sold out Czechoslovakia in the vain hope that it would pacify Nazi aggression, has proved more the rule for twentieth- and twenty-first-century diplomacy than the exception. While Western nations routinely invoke Munich as the preeminent failure of diplomatic nerve—something never to be repeated—these nations continue to make the same mistakes time and again.

The elephant in the room today is Islam. Others, such as Bat Ye'or, have observed the similarities of Western policy in the 1930s and today.[2] Now as then, policymakers and commentators do back flips to avoid the simplest and most cogent explanation for what is going on. Due to their dogged reluctance to relinquish the false assumptions on which their worldview is based, they cannot recognize that they are witnessing the resurgence of a fundamentally violent and expansionary ideology. The "leading minds" of our time cannot see what ought to be obvious: Muslims who commit political violence do so because they take their religion seriously and have the means and opportunity to put it into practice. Not only do the Islamic sources tell us that Muslims are to engage in violence against the infidel, the very terrorists themselves tell us that their motivation is their religion. On what grounds can we reject their claim? Not all

Communists leapt to the barricades in 1917, but those who did were the ones who took Marx's "violent revolution" seriously. Should we be surprised when adherents of a violent ideology commit violence in that ideology's name? To be surprised is to assume that one's own mores, goals, and principles are universally shared—a comforting if totally unwarranted presumption. The pampered diplomats, academics, and politicians today—our "leaders"—have been strongly conditioned to treat any problem that arises as susceptible to the standard gamut of policy options acceptable in a multicultural, politically-correct age. The West today has a superabundance of highly educated, highly intelligent analysts and commentators, with unprecedented amounts of information at their fingertips, who nonetheless totally fail to see the big picture. Awash in statistics and data, they are guilty of missing the forest for the trees. No one these days with a public platform and its concomitant prestige is likely to stand up and announce that there is a hostile ideology at war with our civilization; that there are millions of potential subversives already living within our borders; that our elites have, up to this point, been completely asleep at the switch; and furthermore that the whole idea that cultures and religions are morally equivalent is nonsense. It is to be hoped that others are still clear-headed enough to grasp the truth.

The Muslim world today stretches from the Atlantic in North Africa to the Pacific islands of Indonesia and is on track in a few generations to eclipse Christianity as the world's most populous religion. It is ethnically and culturally diverse, as all civilizations are. It is untenable to postulate that the danger posed by Islam can be reduced to one of geography, ethnicity, economics, or some other "objective" factor. Though the primacy of Arab culture in Islam is undeniable, it is worth remembering that most Muslims are not Arabs and many Arabs are not Muslims. The problem is with the doctrine, ideas, and practices that make up Islam, full stop. It was a blue-eyed European Muslim, the president of Bosnia, Alija Izetbegovic, who, in his *Islamic Declaration*, reaffirmed the "incompatibility of Islam and non-Islamic systems" and that "there can be no peace or coexistence between the 'Islamic faith' and non-Islamic societies and political institutions."[3] It is of course impossible to ascertain just how many nominal Muslims believe this—or are willing to act on it—but the incompatibility of Islam and non-Islamic systems is not a delusion of a handful of fanatics; it is right out of mainstream, orthodox Islam. The scream of *"Allahu Akbar!"* that brought death to the indigenous peoples of Arabia at the hands of Muhammad has echoed throughout history wherever Islam has gained ascendancy. It was that same scream that transformed the thriving societies of the ancient Mediterranean basin into vast graveyards and slave pools, that ushered in the twentieth-century genocide of the Armenians, and that to this day is the primary instigator of war and terrorism worldwide.

It is plain that not all those who call themselves Muslim today are violent just because Islam is fundamentally violent. If all Muslims took jihad seriously we would not be here discussing the question. There are "bad" Muslims as there are "bad" Christians, Jews, etc.—those who claim the mantle of their faith but who fail, for whatever reason, to live up to its mandates. The factors that inform the strength of an individual's faith and his willingness to act on its precepts are surely as varied as individuals themselves. For those Muslims who genuinely value peace, tolerance, and brotherhood in a secular sense, they must look deep into their religion and, hopefully, jettison it. It is clear that as long as Islam is accepted as a legitimate faith in the world, there will be the ever-present danger that those who claim its mantle will take its holy texts and the example of its Prophet seriously. How many Muslims today are potential jihadists? It is impossible to tell. Yet it is equally impossible to deny that huge numbers of Muslims throughout both the House of Islam and the House of War understand the violent essence of their faith. Some understand well enough to preach it, and some understand well enough to act on it. And for those who have lapsed, there is always the chance to rediscover their religious roots. One example of nominal, apparently assimilated Muslims transforming into jihadists occurred in upper New York State in 2002 when six American-born Muslims were arrested for plotting attacks against their countrymen.

> It was through a predominantly Arab-American mosque outside Buffalo, New York, that six American-born Yemeni ethnics—mostly employed, married, and college-educated, all registered Democrats—met a pair of preachers who lured them to an Al Qaeda training camp in Afghanistan and a meeting with Osama bin Laden. A journalist who visited the young men's hometown of Lackawanna, New York, described the Al Qaeda trainees as "the cool, assimilated guys in the community." The FBI agent who elicited their first confession—from a member of the group who had been intercepted in Bahrain—recalled in a Frontline interview, "[W]hen we got on the plane on our way to the States, and he met the case agents from Buffalo, one of his biggest concerns

[was], 'How are the Buffalo Bills doing?' That tells me that he really likes what he has here." These youths had experienced an integrated, American Islamic cultural environment that condoned suicide bombings in Israel as surely as it cheered the home football team. When a local Al Qaeda preacher and his Saudi colleague sought to recruit them, they apparently did so by building on the moral foundation that formed the bedrock of their religious environment—by asking them to take a short walk from the dominion of truce to the dominion of war.[4]

Here is the problem of Muslims living in the House of War in a nutshell: those who still identify as Muslim retain the potential to reawaken to the call of jihad even after they have apparently assimilated. The insidiousness of the danger is evident. And as the Islamic presence in Western countries continues to grow in power and confidence, it will be easier and easier for "moderate" or lapsed Muslims to side with the jihadists.

> Sura 9:38. O you who believe! What is the matter with you, that when you are asked to march forth in the Cause of Allah (i.e., Jihad) you cling heavily to the earth? Are you pleased with the life of this world rather than the Hereafter? But little is the enjoyment of the life of this world as compared with the Hereafter.

As in a Christian paradigm, there is the ever-present threat that those who call themselves Christians will eschew the materialist world, turn the other cheek, and love their neighbor, so in an Islamic paradigm there is the danger that complacent Muslims will heed the call of Allah and take up arms against the unbeliever. While it is the *lapsed* Christian who is the greater danger to his fellow man, it is the *devout* Muslim. Thus, it seems that the only hope for lasting peace is to get Muslims to leave their faith, to reject the tenets of Islam, and to become something else compatible with Western society. The overriding problem, however, is that the West, especially Europe, lacks a compelling worldview capable of challenging Islam on the religious/ideological battlefield. For Muslims in the West to abandon allegiance to jihad and Sharia law, there must be a strong competitor to Islam, an alternative religion or ideology that addresses the same problems of existence and right conduct but that offers very different—yet equally compelling—answers. In much of the West, however, there is no longer any such competitor. Mervyn Hiskett observes the following about his own country, Great Britain, but which certainly applies to other European nations as well:

> The fact is, multicultural . . . Britain has failed because the multiculturalists have failed to understand the nature of Islam. What they offer is a gallimaufry of humanist ideas, and some highly selective comparative religion, shorn of all "irrational" elements, for which an unhallowed relativism, not a passionate accession of faith and a blinding encounter with divinity, is the premise. This is defended as "an ability to cope with the uncertainty posed by pluralism." In fact, it is an attempt to extinguish the sacerdotal. It may seem admirable in the fashionable context of liberal doubt. But what the multiculturalists forget—or have never understood—is that the equation is altogether one-sided. For on the Islamic side there is neither doubt nor pluralism, and only very limited

tolerance. If one confronts this pallid rationalist suspension of belief with the fiery afflatus of transcendental conviction, there is little doubt which will win. All multiculturalism does is to enable the Muslims to run rings around their trusting multiculturalist and inter-faith well wishers, in the business of bending the British education system to their will.[5]

It is in the spirit rather than the body that the modern West shows itself wanting. The material resources of Europe and the Americas far eclipse those of the Islamic world. In a conventional fight, the West, or even America leading a small coalition, must easily prevail over any collection of Islamic adversaries. But it is not massive Muslim hosts threatening to overrun the cities of Europe that is the problem. Through decades of immigration, the Europeans are now confronted with large, urban, Muslim populations that, contrary to any multicultural paradigm, have retained or rediscovered their native faith and are beginning to act on its principles. Pluralist, post-Christian Europe, while materially robust, is spiritually enfeebled and can offer no answer to the fervor of religious belief that still runs strong through much of the Islamic faithful. While their ancestors rallied to the Cross and what it represented, today's Western Europeans possess no unifying faith that can galvanize the remedial action so badly needed to address the growth of Islam in their own countries. While many Muslims have embraced secular European society, the persistent spiritual vacuum in post-Christian Europe leaves their more religiously-inclined brethren with nowhere to go but their native faith with its attendant dangers.

Arnold Toynbee argued that great civilizations do not die, they commit suicide. Indeed, it seems the West has been slowly committing suicide by abandoning those ideas and traditions (Christianity, limited government, etc.) that for centuries have made it what it is. However, in order for a civilization to collapse, it must be replaced or overthrown by some competitor. In the absence of a vigorous alternative, a dying civilization may wobble along, slowly losing its grip on life, perhaps indefinitely. As in the case of Rome, it takes some outside force, the proverbial barbarians at the gates, to nail the coffin shut. In the case of the modern West, one wonders if the barbarians have now arrived.

Though the Islamic world is no longer unified as it was under the Arab, Persian, or Turkish empires, its national-political divisions (and even its religious ones such as the Sunni-Shia divide) in no way render it innocuous. Today, the primary danger (after terrorism itself) is not from Muslim armies threatening to engulf Europe, Russia, and India, but from the gradual transformation of non-Islamic societies into Islamic ones. The Muslim world need never achieve political unity for it to weaken, perhaps fatally, Western civilization. Though in the twentieth century the Communist world suffered from various divisions, it remained an implacable enemy, and the same holds true of the Muslim world today. Communism was a formidable foe, but Islam is much more so. Communism was a secular religion whose active life spanned less than a century, that claimed followers in the millions, and whose objective of a workers' utopia was ultimately shown to be empirically impossible. Islam, however, is a revealed religion that has been active for nearly fourteen centuries, that has claimed billions of followers, and that promises a heavenly paradise for those who fight and die in its cause. Confronted with such an enemy, the only option is to ensure that the Islamic world remains in a state of permanent weakness and that it cannot spread to areas of strength. The alternative is to sit and wait to be overwhelmed.

## LOSING GROUND

In an ironic way, we ought to be grateful that Muslim terrorists have opened some eyes to the growing danger Islam poses. Shorn of terrorism, Islam would still constitute an implacable enemy. Many Muslims argue against the use of terrorism because of its potential to galvanize the far more powerful West into decisive action. Such long-term Muslim thinkers argue that, given cultural and demographic trends, Islam will achieve its aims without the need for terrorism. In Europe, for example, substantial parts of major cities are already dominated by Muslim communities and the demographic outlook is bleak: Muslim birth rates in Europe far exceed those of the native European populations, which have been below replacement levels for decades. If current trends continue, Western Europe will be majority Muslim before the end of the century. (The most popular name for boys in Brussels today is Muhammad.)[6] As the Muslim minority in Europe (and North America) grows, it will press ever harder on the native culture to bow to its demands. Eventually we can expect replays of the civil wars in Lebanon and Bosnia, formerly non-Muslim countries in which the indigenous, non-Muslim populations were overwhelmed by faster-growing Muslim minorities, to take place in Western Europe. When Islamic communities are strong enough, they are directed by their theology to take up arms and impose Islamic law; when they are weak, they bide their time. The major conflicts in the post-Cold War world reflect societies at the tipping point: Israel/Palestine, Kashmir, Thailand, East Timor, Ivory

Coast, Nigeria, Sudan, Kosovo, Chechnya, the Philippines, etc., where Muslims have waged jihad to recapture formerly Islamic territory, to consolidate Muslim rule, or to bring Islamic law to a non-Muslim society.

The Muslim world is now reawakening from several decades—one might argue several centuries—of slumber in which it was overwhelmingly dominated by the Western powers. The material situation of much of the Muslim world has been greatly improved thanks to its oil reserves, and there is surely some irony in the West actively subsidizing those nations actively desiring its destruction. Even so, the rise of the West and the concomitant decline of Islamic civilization that began in the Middle Ages might very well have continued into the twentieth and twenty-first centuries. One might imagine, for example, that with the totalitarian dangers of National Socialism and Soviet Communism a thing of the past, the Europeans might now get down to the seriously difficult business of dealing with Islam, which they had been doing for about half a millennium before they started warring primarily with themselves in the sixteenth and seventeenth centuries. Although Europe certainly possesses the material wherewithal to resist Islamic expansion, it has demonstrated a total lack of will to do so. Instead, the European political and intellectual culture is dominated by a kind of self-hatred in which the "crimes" of the West's past—imperialism, racism, capitalism, arms sales, Christian missionizing, etc.—cut off at the knees any attempt to rally Europe to the cause of its own self-preservation. Whatever their hand-wringing over terrorism and fanaticism, European elites have shown no stomach for a fight with Islam.

Put tersely, Islam is conquering Europe. Not by force of

arms, through spectacular sieges or battles as when it fought its way into France, Central Europe, and Russia in centuries past, but through the permeation of European society by individual Muslims who, to greater or lesser degrees, desire the replacement of secular European civilization with Islam. It would be inappropriate to say "infiltration" inasmuch as the process is occurring in broad daylight with the active connivance of the European governments—even if they may fail to appreciate the end to which it is heading. (The post–World War II Islamization of Europe has been exhaustively detailed by Bat Ye'or in *Eurabia: The Euro-Arab Axis*.) While it seems unimaginable that Europe should someday no longer be European—that France should no longer be French, Germany German, or Holland Dutch—that is precisely what is happening and with a speed that ought to be alarming. Estimates suggest that the Muslim population in Europe will double in twenty years, while the native Caucasian population declines. Major demographic changes often bring turmoil to a society, but in this case the growing minority carries with it not only its own cultural differences but a militant ideology directly opposed to the civil society around it.

The huge welfare states of Europe have become addicted to cheap foreign labor and have no means to support their rapidly aging, barren populations apart from huge numbers of (mainly Muslim) immigrants. European civilization has hooked itself up to a suicide machine that with each passing day leaks another dose of deadly fluid into its veins.

What is occurring in Western Europe has occurred at other times in other places with calamitous results. Of course, all of the Islamic world today comprises territories in which other civilizations once flourished but which succumbed—sometimes

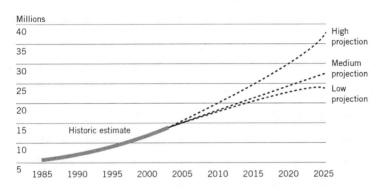

# EU: Estimated and Projected Muslim Population, 1985–2025

Source: Based on a variety of diplomatic and media reporting as well as government, academic, and other sources.

Estimated EU Muslim population through 2025. (National Intelligence Council.)

quickly, sometimes gradually—to the genocidal effects of jihad and dhimmitude. But there are also more recent, telling examples, such as Lebanon. Until the 1970s, Lebanon was governed predominantly by Christians; Beirut, regarded by many as the jewel of the eastern Mediterranean, another Riviera, was a favorite holiday resort for western Europeans. But as the number of Muslims in Lebanon grew, the Christians' hold on power began to slip. With the arrival of the PLO and Yasir Arafat from Tunisia in 1969, the Christian government lost control and the country degenerated into civil war. In a few years, the jewel of the eastern Mediterranean was transformed into a heap of smoking rubble. While the political and military situation was complicated (as all civil wars are), it should not be at all surprising that a Muslim community took up arms to establish political hegemony in accordance with its religious beliefs.

The Balkan Wars of the 1990s offer other recent examples—also complicated, of course—of efforts by Muslims to achieve political control of non-Islamic territories. The prevalent misrepresentation of the Balkan wars as the consequence of Serbian aggression served then (and serves now) to further Muslim designs of setting up the first Islamic states in Europe, namely, Bosnia and Kosovo. As the Bosnian Muslims seceded from Yugoslavia in the early 1990s in an attempt to set up an Islamic state, so the Kosovar Muslims have managed to do so in setting up an independent Kosovo (with Western help). The irony is that none of this would have been possible without the West's sympathy and connivance, as Diane Johnstone (*Fool's Crusade*) has devastatingly revealed.

As bizarre as it may sound, from the 1980s to the attacks of 2001, the West, led by America, pursued a basically pro-jihadist foreign policy: supporting the Mujahideen in Afghanistan against the Soviet Union in the late 1970s and 1980s, the Muslims in Bosnia in the 1990s, the terrorist KLA (Kosovo Liberation Army) in Kosovo, and to a lesser degree the jihadists in Chechnya against post-Soviet Russia. Indeed, US foreign policy even now is directed at encouraging popular movements in the Islamic world at the expense of traditional, more secular, dictatorships. One point apparently overlooked is that the popular opposition in Muslim countries is invariably, uncompromisingly Islamic. However corrupt and unreliable the dictatorships of the Arab Islamic countries have proved, they are vastly preferable to full-blown Islamic regimes dedicated to jihad and Sharia law. What Khomeini did in Iran in 1979 the United States may wind up accomplishing on a much broader scale: replacing unpopular, secular, authoritarian regimes with more popular, Islamic, totalitarian ones. The US deposition of Iraqi dictator Saddam Hussein in 2003 is a case in point. Hussein, a Sunni, presided over a Shia-majority nation and was obliged to balance competing religious groups, including Christian, affording them a modicum of freedom. With his ouster, the way was paved for a popular Shia government, which systematically excluded Sunni representatives and opened the door for what has been effectively a low-grade civil war that has claimed tens and perhaps hundreds of thousands of lives since 2003. The small Christian minority that enjoyed protection under Hussein has been virtually wiped out. The most recent and dramatic result of the "democratization" of Iraq has been the rise of the murderous Sunni "Islamic State" in the north and west of the country, which claims the mantle of the Caliphate and which has called on Muslims everywhere to wage jihad against the infidel powers and those Muslims who make peace with them. Now, the US is intent on doing to Syria what it has done to Iraq. The US plan of arming supposed Syrian moderates to fight "extremists" betrays an utter lack of realism (in civil wars, arms will inevitably find their way into the hands of those who most want them, i.e., the "extremists") and a profound ignorance of Islam. (There can hardly be a clearer case of throwing gasoline on a fire than sending arms to Muslim insurgents). The current US binge of pushing democracy upon the House of Islam may yet prove one of the most disastrous political obsessions in modern history.

We are now witnessing the reemergence of Islam as a leading force on the stage of world politics, in which allegiances are increasingly extra-national. A true-believing Muslim living in, say, London, is likely to be a Muslim first rather than an

Englishman; his allegiance is first to his coreligionists and their cause—the bringing of Sharia law to the territory in which he lives and to the rest of the House of War. Contrary to the theory that Muslims will assimilate into Western societies over successive generations, it is now evident that the children and grandchildren of Muslim immigrants identify more as Muslims and less as Westerners than their elders. The Muslims who committed the July 7, 2005, London bombings were all native Britons. The rioters in France in the fall of 2005 were not so much immigrants as the French-born children of immigrants. The upshot is that the Western nation-state system is dissolving in the solvent of an Islamic revival. When the history of the West is written, it may be that the events that now define modern Western society—the American War of Independence, the French Revolution, the World Wars, the rise and fall of Soviet Communism—are relegated to footnotes in the colossal millennium-and-a-half-long contest between the House of Islam and the House of War.

We must learn from history and not be tempted to believe that our generation is immune to the forces that have in the past caused conflict with lamentable regularity. We should remember that the nations today that we reflexively think of as Muslim—Turkey, Iraq, Iran, Indonesia, Syria, Egypt, Algeria, etc.—were once thriving, advanced, non-Muslim civilizations. It can happen again. Who would have thought, for example, that Sarajevo, the beautiful, westernized European city that hosted the Olympic Winter Games in 1984, would find itself torn to pieces by a Muslim-led civil war in less than ten years time? Similarly, today it seems unimaginable that, say, Amsterdam, Paris, or London should in ten or twenty years decompose into urban fighting—it is a picture that violates all sense of normalcy—but of course snipers in Sarajevo and shattered buildings in Lebanon did as well.

The question facing the West is whether it can tolerate what happened in Beirut, Mogadishu, Kosovo, Sarajevo, and Beslan happening in Rotterdam, Brussels, Paris, Marseilles, Malmo, and London. The rock-throwing, car-burning "youths" that threw hundreds of French cities into chaos in the fall of 2005 are but the thin end of the wedge that will in due course break out into open civil war. So far, nothing is being done to forestall the coming disaster. How the coming war unfolds will depend on the rapidity with which European Islamic forces mobilize and whether the current national governments will manage to organize a defense. Given the more centralized character of most European governments (as opposed to America's federal system), should those governments persist in their policy of appeasement, there may be no alternative locus of power to which the marginalized European populace can rally. Should America declare herself in the conflict (as one hopes she will), she may by that time find no functional European regime to support. Indeed, it may even transpire that Muslim activists manage to co-opt the current regimes intact with the result that the transition from secular to Islamic governance is entirely progressive. One point of significance: should the current experiment of EU consolidation hold together long enough, it may provide the skeleton for a future European Islamic superstate. In short, the political future of Europe is at best uncertain, but one thing is clear: the calling cards that Islam has left throughout history—assassinations, massacres, rapes, desecrations—are on the rise.

America, for all her willingness to fight "terror," is starting to fall into the same trap as Europe. There are already sizable Muslim populations in the United States—in New Jersey, the environs of Detroit, Los Angeles, and elsewhere—and she shows no signs of curtailing Muslim immigration or organization. Her leaders seem as hypnotized by the siren's ballad of multiculturalism as Europe's. But sooner or later America is likely to be faced with a colossal geostrategic problem: an Islamicized Europe, perhaps intact, perhaps fragmented and depleted from civil war. The saving grace for the non-Islamic world has for centuries been the inability of the House of Islam to mobilize effectively around a single center. More than once has the West been saved by infighting among rival Islamic powers. Political fragmentation continues to be the hallmark of the Islamic world, but it is at least possible that a charismatic Islamic leader could unite much of the Umma into a formidable coalition, one that could someday include much of Western Europe.

America's freedom of action will be further hampered by the likelihood of her own domestic Muslim population climbing through the millions, which will resist—politically or otherwise—efforts to contain Islam abroad. The violent reactions of Western Muslims to Salman Rushdie's 1988 novel *The Satanic Verses*, to allegations that American interrogators at Guantanimo Bay mishandled a Koran, to the accidental electrocution of two Muslim boys being pursued by French police, to the publication of cartoons satirizing the Prophet Muhammad, etc., are but small-scale examples of what we can expect to become a much more widespread phenomenon: the holding hostage of Western governments by their burgeoning Muslim minorities. America has so far escaped the riots experienced by Europe not, as is likely, because American Muslims are somehow more docile, but because in America the Muslim community is still too small and weak to engage in open violence. But that is changing.

Already in America we are witnessing the proliferation of petty jihadists who, apparently unassociated with any significant network, are taking matters into their own hands. Take, for example, John Allen Mohammed and John Lee Malvo, two converts to Islam who perpetrated the Washington, DC, beltway sniper attacks in the fall of 2002 that killed ten, and Mohammed Reza Taheri-azar, an Iranian student at UNC Chapel Hill, who injured nine after deliberately driving his SUV into a crowd of his fellow students. "After the incident, he seemed singularly pleased with himself, smiling and waving to crowds after a court appearance on Monday, at which he explained that he was 'thankful for the opportunity to spread the will of Allah.'"[7] We can expect a lot more of this sort of thing in the future. And the American press and law enforcement have consistently shown themselves unwilling to confront the Islamic nature of these crimes. The sniper "John Allen Mohammed" became "John Allen Williams"— his name before his conversion; the July 4, 2002, shooting at the El Al ticket counter at Los Angeles Airport by Muslim Hesham Mohamed Ali Hadayet was initially not considered terrorism by the FBI; the murder and near beheading of Ariel Sellouk, a Jew, in Houston, Texas, by his friend Mohammed Ali Alayed in 2003, was proclaimed by authorities as lacking a religious motivation even though Alayed had recently begun attending a radical mosque and was found there immediately following the crime.[8] Perhaps the most appalling episode to date was that of US Army Major Nidal Malik Hasan, who, brandishing firearms and shouting "Allahu Akbar!" murdered thirteen of his fellow soldiers and wounded thirty-two at Fort Hood, Texas in 2009. In the midst of the government's hand-wringing over whether to label the massacre "terrorism" or "workplace violence," Hasan released documents that included the following statement: "There is an inherent and irreconcilable conflict . . . in an American Democracy 'we the people' govern according to what 'we the people' think is right or wrong; even if it specifically goes against what All-Mighty God commands." On most of the documents could be found "SoA" for "Soldier of Allah."[9] Apparently for Major Hasan, not even the bonds of comradeship with his fellow soldiers nor his Hippocratic oath (Major Hasan was an army psychiatrist) could overcome his allegiance to the commands of his Islamic faith. Since even the attacks of September 11, in all their monstrous vividness, failed to shake loose the prejudice that Islam is a religion of peace, one shudders to imagine what sort of event may be required.

# 9

# WHAT IS TO BE DONE?

BEFORE WE CAN ACT PROPERLY, WE must think properly. This book and its parallel documentary, *Islam: What the West Needs to Know*, seek to provide tools for Westerners to understand Islam and the danger it poses. The first task for the West must be to reclassify Islam as a political system with religious aspects rather than simply as a religion. Islam is an alternative form of government in competition with other forms that seeks to weaken and, ultimately, replace them. The growth of Islam in the West is a classic case of *imperium in imperio*, a state within a state, which compromises the ability of the secular state to maintain order and liberty. Under the guise of religious freedom, Muslim activists will subvert Western societies, first politically and then by force. Islam must not be given the protected status of a religion precisely because it does not recognize the separation of religion and politics on which Western-style government and religious freedom are based. Any recognition of legitimacy must be reciprocal: it is illogical—and suicidal—for Western governments to regard Islam as a legitimate religion when Islam is unwilling to recognize the legitimacy of those same governments.

Islam is concerned with the question of jihad and the drafting and the mobilisation of the entire *Umma* into one body to defend the right cause with all its strength than any other ancient or modern system of living {*sic*}, whether religious or civil. The verses of the Qur'an and the Sunnah of Muhammad (PBUH {Peace Be Unto Him}) are overflowing with all these noble ideals and they summon people in general (with the most eloquent expression and the clearest exposition) to jihad, to warfare, to the armed forces, and all means of land and sea fighting.[1]

Any civil society is based on its members extending to one another the benefit of the doubt. In a legal setting, this translates to the presumption of innocence. It is to our credit that we want to see in others the same aspirations and principles of right conduct as ourselves. A society in which its members do not give each other the benefit of the doubt, in which everyone instinctively mistrusts and suspects everyone else, will soon degenerate into anarchy or repression. It is this noble instinct of tolerance that has permitted huge numbers of Muslims to immigrate to Western countries and live largely undisturbed. But, as is increasingly clear, Western tolerance is being exploited by Islamic intolerance. Live and let live, as we have seen, is certainly not an Islamic principle. Our magnanimity is being used against us.

It would seem natural here to suggest specific remedies to be taken by the West to counter the growing danger from Islam, but I believe that is beyond the scope of this book. I do not want to pick a fight over policy that could distract from the central point that Islam is intrinsically and ineradicably violent. Until the problem is more widely recognized, attempts to foster a remedy are surely futile. What must happen first is for the public at large to become aware of the danger and to insist that their hitherto negligent representatives take it seriously. We can, however, outline in general terms a strategy that would help to minimize the risk from Islamic violence at home and prevent orthodox Islam with its attendant aspirations for jihad and Sharia from expanding overseas.

To ask the question of how the Islamic danger may be dealt with, however, evokes the worrying possibility that the cure could be as bad as the disease. To what lengths would state power need to go to safeguard us from such a formidable danger? Would declaring Islam an open enemy precipitate even greater violence? Would further domestic security measures strangle civil liberties? Would we not effectively inaugurate a global war with no plausible scenario for victory? Such questions are not easily dismissed, but I believe they are also not insuperable.

The general policy that the West and the rest of the non-Islamic world must pursue is one of containment, of holding Islamic influence in check and preventing it from moving to areas of greater strength, namely, preventing it from reaching dangerous levels of organization within Western countries. The basic elements of the containment strategy were outlined by George Kennan in his treatment of Soviet Communism during the Cold War, the basic principles of which are to prevent the adversary from expanding his sphere of control while refraining as much as possible from offensive actions likely to prove costly. (Needless to say, during the Cold War the containment strategy was carried out with a high degree of imperfection.) Contrary to current US-led interventions to democratize the Islamic world, which only stir up more trouble and antagonize those who might otherwise sympathize with a considered anti-Islamic policy, the West should seek to contain Islam within its current boundaries while curtailing its growing influence in Western societies. Democratization in the Islamic world invariably means Islamization. Quasi-secular dictatorships, however distasteful, have proven far more tolerant and amenable to Western interests than full-blown Islamic regimes bent on Sharia and jihad. Containment at home would entail rescinding Islam's protected status as a religion and reclassifying it as a political ideology. Law enforcement would thus be permitted greater freedom of action in forestalling specifically Islamic violence while reducing the need for the larger surveillance state that scrutinizes citizens indiscriminately.

A key pillar of any effective policy of containment would be for the West to bury the hatchet with other countries who themselves face an Islamic threat. Since the end of the Cold War, the US-led West has shown a remarkable proclivity for retaining and even augmenting its anti-Soviet/anti-Russian policies, which have served to alienate one of the leading nations in the struggle with Islam. With a population that is roughly fifteen percent Muslim, Islam looms large on the Russian political stage. Since the fall of Soviet Communism, Islamic terror attacks have claimed the lives of hundreds of Russians. Furthermore, Russia has shown herself willing and able to assist the West in its fight against Islamic terrorism, such as supplying much needed logistical support to the American operations against the Taliban in Afghanistan. What Russia has got in return is the continuing expansion of NATO to her very borders (in contravention of Western promises over the reunification of Germany) and economic and political isolation over matters of

Crimea and Eastern Ukraine that involve no evident Western strategic interest. Indeed, Russia amounts to something of a success story as a Christian country that has managed to absorb a very large Muslim population with a minimum of internal divisions. Russia has survived thanks at least in part to her continued self-consciousness as a Christian nation-state in which her historic religion is central to her cultural and political life. (So far, the city of Moscow has permitted the construction of four mosques for its two million Muslims, while boasting three hundred churches.) Whereas Western Europe has abandoned its Christian roots, Russia, after suffering seventy years of official atheism, is cultivating hers. The reasons for the ongoing Western antipathy toward Russia are beyond the scope of this book, but both sides would do well to put their differences aside and make common cause against the burgeoning Islamic danger both within and without their borders.

For those of us aware of the violent nature of Islam, we must resolve to speak candidly what we know to be true about Islam, what it is and what it has done. We must not be cowed by charges of racism or Islamophobia; we must not be afraid of ridicule or ostracism by elites whose careers have been made peddling soft, comfortable fictions; and we must not be afraid even of paying the ultimate price. Clearly, Islam's true believers are willing to kill and die for their cause. If some of us are not at least willing to die for ours, we are surely lost. From the bloody deeds of Muhammad to the Armenian Genocide to the terrorist jihadists of today, we must speak the truth candidly. We must also, I believe, while witnessing to the violent nature of Islam, continue to treat individual Muslims with courtesy and respect and maintain, as much as possible, the civil society that we value and seek to uphold.

Having identified the enemy, the second crucial task for the West is to identify itself. Defining what the West is—what is unique to it and what distinguishes it—is prerequisite to any concerted defense. Rallying in the name of freedom, democracy, tolerance, etc. isn't going to cut it; such abstractions are just as readily used by Muslim activists in defense of their aims. Unhappily, there is a great deal of commonality among the aims of Islam and contemporary Western policies, both of which functionally undermine traditional Western society, Christianity, and the integrity of the nation-state. In order to survive, the West will have to rediscover those ideas, traditions, and principles that constitute its essential and non-negotiable characteristics. As during the Cold War, articulating what are the pillars of Western civilization and how they may be defended against a global enemy is the great challenge for Western minds—at least for those that value their heritage or their survival.

But even a cursory attempt to define the West evokes the unhappy possibility that much of it may already be lost. The unwillingness of much of Europe, for example, to perpetuate itself, even if only biologically, hardly bespeaks a willingness to make the sacrifices necessary to counter a foe as determined as Islamic jihad. The logic of European postmodernism has taken its toll: the central cause of Europe's incapacity to mount a defense is that Europe no longer believes that it has anything worth defending. Everything that once made Europe great and distinguished it from other civilizations—overseas expansion, Christianity, superior cultural achievement—has been systematically marginalized. Apart from liquor and sausages, the Europe of today has no good answer to the question of *why* it should prevent its Islamization. If European civilization really is as bad as relativist intellectuals claim, why on earth should anyone lift a finger to defend it? And if there are going to be hardly any Europeans around in a few generations anyway, one may as well eat, drink, and be merry before the ship finally goes down.

A voice from a contemporary Western-inspired war zone, northern Iraq, pithily states the magnitude and urgency of the problem. There, where the "Islamic State" pursues a policy of jihad and religious cleansing, the leader of one of the few remaining Christian communities, Amel Nona, the Chaldean Catholic Archbishop of Mosul, offers a lament and a warning:

> Our sufferings today are the prelude of those you, Europeans and Western Christians, will also suffer in the near future. I lost my diocese. The physical setting of my apostolate has been occupied by Islamic radicals who want us converted or dead. But my community is still alive. Please, try to understand us. Your liberal and democratic principles are worth nothing here. You must consider again our reality in the Middle East, because you are welcoming in your countries an ever growing number of Muslims. Also you are in danger. You must take strong and courageous decisions, even at the cost of contradicting your principles. You think all men are equal, but that is not true: Islam does not say that all men are equal. Your values are not their values. If you do not understand this soon enough, you will become the victims of the enemy you have welcomed in your home.[2]

## VOICES FROM THE PAST

We began this inquiry by observing the public complacency of Western leaders vis-à-vis Islam. It is tempting to imagine that, even while they gurgle out their blithe proclamations of Islam's peacefulness, in the secret, smoke-filled chambers of power, *they really know better* and are hard at work saving the world from Islamic expansion—a conspiracy of virtue, as it were. Such a possibility cannot be conclusively disproved, of course. But those who take comfort in such fantasies should be reminded that the graveyards of history are full of politicians too clever by half: men who thought that, through their special abilities, they could reconcile expedient public positions in contradiction with the facts. Perhaps the British people relied on Neville Chamberlain to "know better"—we know where that got them. It will come to no good if Western leaders continue to mischaracterize Islam publicly, whether they think they know better or not. Even if they really appreciate the threat of Islam, they may still be clinging to the dream that Islam will, in time, become something it is not—the much-vaunted "religion of peace." We must remind them that for fourteen hundred years Islam has been what it is: violent, expansionary, tyrannical, bloody. For Islam to transform itself into something peaceful, it would have to jettison two things: Muhammad and the Koran. The notion that it shall be us—our generation—that shall turn Islam into something it is not nor has ever been can only be regarded as a testament to monumental hubris.

> Volume 9, Book 92, Number 382. *Narrated Abdullah:* The best talk (speech) is Allah's Book (The Quran), and the best way is the way of Muhammad, and the worst matters are

the heresies (those new things which are introduced into the religion); and whatever you have been promised will surely come to pass, and you cannot escape (it).

The systematic blindness of Western politicians, journalists, and academics, almost regardless of background or party affiliation, is indeed puzzling. There is no easy explanation for it. It is not obvious why, at least in principle, a statesman in a Western, non-Islamic context, cannot stand up and begin to educate his constituents in sober and reasonable tones as to the true nature of Islam. But to acknowledge a fundamental division between Islam and the rest of the world would violate the reigning multicultural paradigm and, even more so, the dominant program, evident at so many levels, of globalization. While occasionally someone may stick his neck out against the assumptions of multiculturalism, few question the logic or inevitability of globalization, which indeed must entail the amalgamation of cultures and religions and which could never tolerate the idea that some cultures and peoples are fundamentally incompatible. Indeed, a policy of containment would strike at the heart of the assumptions of globalization, at the whole possibility of fabricating a unified global society in which all persons, regardless of belief or background, would live as brothers. But why world leaders of every stripe seem hypnotized by the necessity of globalization to the detriment of their own constituents is a lengthy discussion that must wait for another time.

It is surely ironic that, punctuated as our own time has been by spectacular episodes of jihadist violence, awareness of Islam's violent nature has been far greater in times past. The astute nineteenth-century Frenchman who gave us the seminal

*Democracy in America* and *The Old Regime and the Revolution in France*, Alexis de Tocqueville, had this to say:

> I have studied the Koran a great deal, above all because of our position vis-à-vis the Muslim populations in Algeria and throughout the Orient. I came away from that study with the conviction that by and large there have been few religions in the world as deadly to men as that of Muhammad. As far as I can see, it is the principal cause of the decadence so visible today in the Muslim world, and, though less absurd than the polytheism of old, its social and political tendencies are in my opinion infinitely more to be feared, and I therefore regard it as a form of decadence rather than a form of progress in relation to paganism itself.[3]

At a time when the Ottoman Empire was in conspicuous decline, it is significant that de Tocqueville even then discerned that Islam's "social and political tendencies" were "to be feared." He perceived that the danger lies in Islam's inherent doctrines and not in any perversion of them. Americans, too, have proved more clear-headed in times past, even while the danger then was more irritating than acute. In 1786, the future American presidents John Adams and Thomas Jefferson reported on the ongoing threat of piracy to American shipping in the Mediterranean from the Muslim Barbary States of North Africa.

> We took the liberty to make some inquiries concerning the Grounds of their pretensions to make war upon a Nation who had done them no Injury, and observed that we considered all mankind as our Friends who had done us no wrong, nor had given us any provocation. The Ambassador answered

us that it was founded on the Laws of their Prophet, that it was written in their Koran, that all nations who should not have acknowledged their authority were sinners, that it was their right and duty to make war upon them wherever they could be found, and to make slaves of all they could take as Prisoners, and that every Musselman who should be slain in Battle was sure to go to Paradise.[4]

It is surely ironic that America's statesmen of today have shown themselves so unwilling to take a page from two of their most illustrious predecessors on so fundamental a matter.

But perhaps the most cogent modern assessment of Islam was given by the great Roman Catholic historian and polemicist Hilaire Belloc. Writing amidst the lowering skies of the 1930s, when western Europe seemed ready to be engulfed by the twin totalitarianisms of Communism and National Socialism, Belloc perceived that Islam could one day recrudesce as an even greater danger. While decrying the modern attack against Christianity vividly present in his own time, Belloc saw through to even larger historical forces still at work.

> It has always seemed to me possible, and even probable, that there would be a resurrection of Islam and that our sons or our grandsons would see the renewal of that tremendous struggle between the Christian culture and what has been for more than a thousand years its greatest opponent.[5]

The religious bent of Belloc's mind allowed him to perceive that the most powerful historical forces are invariably religious in nature. However weakened materially Islam had become, because it had not lost its doctrinal vitality, he reasoned, because it still possessed a dynamic faith, it remained a source of power and therefore of danger.

> In Islam there has been no such dissolution of ancestral doctrine—or, at any rate, nothing corresponding to the universal break-up of religion in Europe . . .
>
> There is nothing in the Muhammadan civilization itself which is hostile to the development of the scientific knowledge or of mechanical aptitude. . . . There is nothing inherent to Muhammadanism to make it incapable of modern science and modern war. . . . That culture has fallen back in material applications; there is no reason whatever why it should not learn its new lesson and become our equal in all those temporal things which now alone give us our superiority over it—whereas in Faith we have fallen inferior to it.[6]

Simply put, Belloc knew that where there is a will, there is a way, and Islam had retained its will. In Belloc's view, the West's great crime was to have thrown away its religious inheritance in the form of traditional Christianity; whatever the West's material accomplishments, they mattered little if its animating spirit was seeping away. The danger Belloc foresaw was that Islam would regroup from its few centuries' hiatus and return to challenge a West that no longer knew what it was about; a West replete with wealth and gadgets but lacking the moral fortitude to resist. Whatever Islam's contemporary problems—such as technical backwardness and political fragmentation—the student of history Belloc knew that Islam's record of competent, concerted, offensive action was far lengthier and more impressive than its recent problems.

These things being so, the recrudescence of Islam, the possibility of that terror under which we lived for centuries reappearing, and of our civilization again fighting for its life against what was its chief enemy for a thousand years, seems fantastic . . .

I say the suggestions that Islam may re-arise sounds fantastic—but this is only because men are always powerfully affected by the immediate past—one might say that they are blinded by it.[7]

One may criticize Belloc's rather partisan scholarship, but it does seem that in his conclusions he hit the nail on the head. That his awareness of history exceeds ours today is readily illustrated by the following poignant passage:

The last effort they {the Muslims} made to destroy {Western} Christendom was contemporary with the end of the reign of Charles II in England and of his brother James and of the usurper William III. It failed during the last years of the seventeenth century, only just over two hundred years ago. Vienna, as we saw, was almost taken and only saved by the Christian army under the command of the King of Poland on a date that ought to be among the most famous in history—September 11, 1683.[8]

A date made famous once again.

The West must awaken to the fact that it is facing nothing less than the resurgence of the greatest war machine in world history: an ideology that holds the killing of others, the plundering of their wealth, the conquering of their lands, the enslavement of their people, and the destruction of their institutions to be among the highest virtues and the stepping stones to salvation. In the past, the West had to contend with Islam as an alien force from without, as an invader that had to be met on the battlefield. Now, however, the greatest danger from Islam is increasingly from within. The West's ancient adversary has gained a foothold within Western Civilization itself through the West's own moral confusion. This new phase in the struggle with Islam will be played out in the cities of Europe, which in time may yet become new battlefields. Yet it seems that the secular West, having failed to heed the warnings of the past, is determined not to hear the bad news. It is hoping against hope that things are not as bad as they seem. It is hoping that the myriad acts of violence around the world done in the name of Allah are somehow not indicative of "real" Islam. It is hoping that the Muslims in its midst who reject Western civil society and press increasingly hard for the acceptance of Islamic culture and Sharia law are just blowing hot air. It is hoping that Islam—a religion founded by one of history's great warlords, that waged wars of aggression and conquest for a thousand years, that slaughtered and enslaved untold millions, and that today produces terrorism, suicide bombings, hostage-taking, and massacres around the world—that this strange, seething, violent mass is somehow "a religion of peace." Rejecting this fiction and standing up to be counted will determine whether or not we survive the twenty-first century.

# APPENDIX I

# SUGGESTED RESOURCES

## ONLINE

www.chroniclesmagazine.org—Serge Trifkovic's (*The Sword of the Prophet, Defeating Jihad*) primary online venue

www.dar-us-salam.com—Islamic bookstore with free e-Korans and other books

www.dhimmitude.org—Bat Ye'or's (*The Decline of Eastern Christianity under Islam, Eurabia: The Euro-Arab Axis*) primary online venue

www.faithfreedom.org—a superb website administered by ex-Muslims which sets out with cogency and precision the facts about Islam and the plight of apostates

www.jihadwatch.org—Robert Spencer's (*Islam Unveiled, The Myth of Islamic Tolerance*) primary online venue

www.whatthewestneedstoknow.com—Website of the documentary *Islam: What the West Needs to Know*

## BOOKS

Lammens, Henri and Sir E. Denison Ross, *Islam—Beliefs and Institutions*. Routledge Library Editions Vol.16, Islam. Reprinted. New York: Routledge, 2008.

In my view, this is probably the best single book on Islam, though unfortunately it can be rather hard to find. In the first hundred or so pages, Lammens lucidly spells out the major moving parts of Islam. The current myths regarding the "religion of peace" evaporate when exposed to this impartial exposition. Lammens died in 1937, and his pre-war prose is blessedly devoid of the obfuscation and axe-grinding that afflicts many more recent works.

Ishaq, Ibn. *The Life of Muhammad*. Translated by Alfred Guillaume. Oxford University Press, 2002.

For the more patient reader, the Sira is probably the best means of grasping the fundaments of Muhammad and his legacy. The majority of the book is devoted to Muhammad's military campaigns fought from Medina, AD 622–32. Reading the astonishingly bloody details of Muhammad's life—and the fastidiousness with which they were incorporated into the Islamic canon—is probably the most powerful antidote to the falsehood that Islam is a "religion of peace."

Robert Spencer. *Islam Unveiled*. New York, NY: Encounter Books, 2002.

Trifkovic, Serge. *The Sword of the Prophet*. Salisbury, MA: Regina Orthodox Press, 2002.

Warraq, Ibn. *Why I am Not a Muslim*. Amherst, NY: Prometheus Books, 2003.

Three very good books that each capably shatter in a few hundred pages the major myths about Islam, the Koran, Muhammad, jihad, and the origins of Islamic violence.

Ye'or, Bat. *The Decline of Eastern Christianity under Islam*. Madison, NJ: Farleigh Dickinson University Press, 1996.

———. *Islam and Dhimmitude: Where Civilizations Collide*. Madison, NJ: Farleigh Dickinson University Press, 2001.

The foremost scholarly treatments of the history of Islamic jihad in the West and the plight of conquered non-Muslim populations. Bat Ye'or coined the term *dhimmitude* to describe the state of the oppressed, brutalized Christians and Jews who lived under Islamic rule through the centuries. Bat Ye'or's scholarship, probably more than any other, has provided the means for rebutting the persistent myths about Islam and its historical treatment of non-Muslims.

Bostom, Andrew G., ed. *The Legacy of Jihad*. Amherst, NY: Prometheus Books, 2005.

This gigantic tome probably constitutes the most comprehensive indictment of Islam as a violent ideology ever assembled. Detailed eyewitness accounts, extensive exposition from Muslim theologians, and numerous other primary sources provide ample evidence of how extensively Islam's bloody footprints cover history.

Spencer, Robert, ed. *The Myth of Islamic Tolerance*. Amherst, NY: Prometheus Books, 2005.

Another massive collection of evidence and argument that Islam is, and has always been, a belligerent political ideology that seeks the destruction or subjugation of everything that is not itself.

# APPENDIX II

# SURAS OF THE KORAN IN CHRONOLOGICAL ORDER

Various scholars, Muslim and non-Muslim, have endeavored to classify the suras of the Koran in the chronological order in which they were revealed, including Noldeke, Muir, Rodwell, Jalalu'd-Din as-Syuti, and others.[1]

The Egyptian standard edition of the Koran gives the following order with the verses said to date from a different period given in parentheses.[2]

## MECCAN SURAS IN THE ORDER THEY WERE REVEALED:

1. 96
2. 68 (17–33, 48–50 Med.)
3. 73 (10 f., 20 Med.)
4. 74
5. 1
6. 111
7. 81

8. 87

9. 92

10. 89

11. 93

12. 94

13. 103

14. 100

15. 108

16. 102

17. 107

18. 109

19. 105

20. 113

21. 114

22. 112

23. 53

24. 80

25. 97

26. 91

27. 85

28. 106

29. 101

30. 75

31. 104
32. 77 (48 Med.)
33. 50 (38 Med.)
34. 90
35. 86
36. 54 (54–6 Med.)
37. 38
38. 7 (163–70 Med.)
39. 72
40. 36 (45 Med.)
41. 25 (68–70 Med.)
42. 35
43. 19 (58, 71 Med.)
44. 20 (130 f. Med.)
45. 56 (71 f. Med.)
46. 26 (197, 224–7 Med.)
47. 27
48. 28 (52–5 Med., 85 during Hijra)
49. 17 (26, 32 f., 57, 73–80 Med.)
50. 10 (40, 94–6 Med.)
51. 11 (12, 17, 114 Med.)
52. 12 (1-3, 7 Med.)
53. 15

54. 6 (20, 23, 91, 114, 141, 151–3 Med.)

55. 37

56. 31 (27-9 Med.)

57. 34 (6 Med.)

58. 39 (52–4 Med.)

59. 40 (56 f. Med.)

60. 41

61. 42 (23–5, 27 Med.)

62. 43 (54 Med.)

63. 44

64. 45 (14 Med.)

65. 46 (10, 15, 35 Med.)

66. 51

67. 88

68. 18 (28, 83–101 Med.)

69. 16 (126–8 Med.)

70. 71

71. 14 (28 f. Med.)

72. 21

73. 23

74. 32 (16–20 Med.)

75. 52

76. 47

77. 67

78. 70

79. 78

80. 79

81. 82

82. 84

83. 30 (17 Med.)

84. 29 (1–11 Med.)

85. 83 Hijra (emigration from Mecca to Medina)

## MEDINAN SURAS IN THE ORDER THEY WERE REVEALED:

86. 2 (281 later)

87. 8 (30–6 Mec.)

88. 3

89. 33

90. 60

91. 4

92. 99

93. 57

94. 47 (13 during Hijra)

95. 13

96. 55

97. 76

98. 65

99. 98

100. 59

101. 24

102. 22

103. 63

104. 58

105. 18

106. 49

107. 66

108. 44

109. 61

110. 62

111. 48

112. 5

113. 9 (128 f. Mec.)

114. 110

# NOTES

## CHAPTER ONE: OBSCURING THE ISSUE

1. Amir Taheri, *Holy Terror* (Bethesda: Adler & Adler, 1987), 241–43.
2. Mervyn Hiskett, *Some to Mecca Turn to Pray* (St Alban's: Claridge Press, 1993), 125.

## CHAPTER TWO: BAD LANGUAGE

1. "Center for Defense Information Terrorism Project," US State Department, Office of Counterterrorism, April 2005, http://www. state.gov/s/ct/rls/fs/37191.htm.
2. Hiskett, *Some to Mecca Turn to Pray*, 203.

## CHAPTER THREE: THE KORAN

1. Akbar S. Ahmed, *Islam Today: A Short Introduction to the Muslim World* (New York: I. B. Tauris, 1999), 40.
2. Dr. Muhammad Muhsin Khan and Dr. Muhammad Taqi-ud-Din Al-Hilali, trans. *Interpretation of the Meanings of the Noble Quran.* (Riyadh: Dar-us-Salaam, 1996).
3. Ibn Warraq, *What the Koran Really Says* (Amherst: Prometheus, 2002), 24.
4. Ibid., 69.

## CHAPTER FOUR: THE SUNNAH

1. Seyyed Hossein Nasr, *Ideals and Realities in Islam* (New York, NY: George Allen & Unwin, 2011), 39.
2. Khan, Dr. Muhammad Muhsin, "Translation of Sahih Al-Bukhari." http://www.usc.edu/dept/MSA/fundamentals/hadithsunnah/bukhari.
3. Muhammad bin Ishaq. *The Life of Muhammad.* Alfred Guillaume, trans. (Oxford: Oxford University Press, 2004).

4. Anonymous, "Muslim Rape Epidemic in Sweden and Norway—Authorities Look the Other Way," fjordman (blog), February 20, 20015, http://fjordman.blogspot.com/2005/02/muslim-rape-epidemic-in-sweden-and.html; Jamie Glazov, "Symposium: To Rape an Unveiled Woman," Frontpage Magazine, March 7, 2006, http://archive.frontpagemag.com/readArticle.aspx?ARTID=5347.

5. William Montgomery Watt, *Muhammad: Prophet and Statesman* (Oxford: Oxford University Press, 1961), 233.

6. Ibid., 234.

7. Ibid., 230.

8. Ibid., 231.

9. Ibid., 235.

## CHAPTER FIVE: ISLAM UNLEASHED

1. Bat Ye'or, *The Decline of Eastern Christianity under Islam* (Madison: Fairleigh Dickinson University Press, 1996), 271.

2. Ibid., 276–77.

3. Ibid., 281–82.

4. Hiskett, Some to Mecca Turn to Pray, 51.

5. Paul Fergosi, *Jihad in the West: Muslim Conquests from the 7th to the 21st Centuries* (Amherst: Prometheus, 1998), 256–57.

6. Ibid., 321.

## CHAPTER SIX: THE DHIMMI

1. Ye'or, *Decline*, 360.

2. Ibid., 381–83.

3. Serge Trifkovic, *The Sword of the Prophet* (Boston: Regina Orthodox Press, 2002), 113.

4. Ye'or, *Decline*, 295.

5. Ibid., 296.

6. Imam Shaheed Hasan Al-Bana, *Jihad* (London: Prelude, 1997).

7. Hiskett, *Some to Mecca Turn to Pray*, 101.

8. Hugh Fitzgerald, "Islam for Infidels," http://www.jihadwatch.org/ archives/004628.php.

9. Muhammad Taqi Partovi Samzevari quoted in Amir Taheri, *Holy Terror* (Bethesda: Adler & Adler, 1987), 254-55.

## CHAPTER SEVEN: JIHAD IN THE MODERN ERA

1. Peter Balakian, *The Burning Tigris* (New York: HarperCollins, 2003), 130.

2. Ibid., 112.

3. Ibid., 112–13.

4. Ibid., 113–14.

5. Ibid., chs. 5, 14, 15, passim.

6. Ibid., 170.

7. Ibid., 238.

8. Ibid., 338–39.

9. Ibid., 339.

## CHAPTER EIGHT: THE ELEPHANT IN THE ROOM

1. Stephanie Courtois, Nicolas Werth, Jean-Louis Panne, et al., *The Black Book of Communism* (Boston: Harvard University Press, 1999).

2. Ye'or, "Beyond Munich" in Robert Spencer, *The Myth of Islamic Tolerance* (Amherst: Prometheus, 2005), 283.

3. Alija Izetbegovic, *Islamic Declaration* (Sarajevo: Bosnia, 1990), 22. http://www.srpska-mreza.com/library/facts/alija.html.

4. Joseph Braude, "Moderate Muslims and Their Radical Leaders" in the *NewRepublic*, 27 February 2006, http://www.newrepublic.com/article/moderate-muslims-and-their-radical-leaders.

5. Hiskett, *Some to Mecca Turn to Pray*, 309.

6. Lowell Ponte, "Goodbye Europe" in *Frontpagemag.com*, March 28, 2006, http://archive.frontpagemag.com/readArticle.aspx?ARTID=5043.

7. Robert Spencer, "Tarheel Jihad" in *Frontpagemag.com*, March 8, 2006, http://archive.frontpagemag.com/readArticle.aspx?ARTID=5297.

8. Robert Spencer, "Terror Denial" in *Frontpagemag.com*, March 6, 2005, http://archive.frontpagemag.com/readArticle.aspx?ARTID=8701; and Pipes, "Denying [Islamist] Terrorism" in the *New York Sun*, February 8, 2005, http://www.danielpipes.org/2396/denying-islamist-terrorism.

9. Catherine Hedge and Pamela Brown, "Hassan Sends Writings to Fox News ahead of Fort Hood Shooting Trial," August 1, 2013, http://www.foxnews.com/politics/2013/08/01/hasan-sends-writings-ahead-fort-hood-shooting-trial.

## CHAPTER NINE: WHAT IS TO BE DONE?

1. Al-Bana, Imam Shaheed Hasan Al-Bana, *Jihad* (London: Prelude, 1997).

2. Robert Spencer, "Exiled Archbishop of Mosul: 'Our sufferings today are the prelude of those you, Europeans and Western Christians, will also suffer in the near future," *Jihad Watch*, August 21, 2014, http://www.jihadwatch.org/2014/08/exiled-archbishop-of-mosul-our-sufferings-today-are-the-prelude-of-those-you-europeans-and-western-christians-will-also-suffer-in-the-near-future.

3. Tocqueville, *Oeuvres*, 69.

4. Adams and Jefferson, "Quotes from the Founding Fathers" in *USDOJ and Government Watch*.

5. Hilaire Belloc, *The Great Heresies* (Rockford: Tan Books and Publishers, 1991), 73.

6. Ibid., 76–77.

7. Ibid., 75 –76.

8. Ibid., 70–71.

## APPENDIX II: SURAS OF THE KORAN

1. Edward Sell, *The Historical Development of the Qur'an*. Facsimile Edition, People International (Tunbridge Wells, England, 1989), http://www.muham madanism.org/Canon_Sell/Quran/default.htm.

2. Vernon Richards, *Islam Undressed*. E-book, 2005, http://www.scribd.com/doc/1035244/Islam-Undressed#scribd.

# GLOSSARY

*Abu Bakr*—first "rightly-guided" Caliph; father of Aisha, Muhammad's favorite wife; ruled AD 632–34 after Muhammad's death.

*Ali*—fourth and last "rightly-guided" Caliph; ruled AD 656–61, succeeded Uthman.

*Allah*—literally "God"; Arabic Christians also worship "Allah" but an Allah of a very different sort.

*Allahu Akhbar*—"God is Great (-est)"; term of praise; war cry of Muslims.

*Ansar*—"aiders" or "helpers"; Arabian tribesmen allied with Muhammad and the early Muslims.

*Badr*—first major battle fought by Muhammad and the Muslims against the Quraish tribe of Mecca.

*Caliph*—title of the ruler or leader of the *Umma* (global Muslim community); the head of the former Islamic Empire; the title was abolished by Kemal Attaturk in 1924 following the breakup of the Ottoman Empire and the founding of modern Turkey.

*dar al-harb*—"House of War"; territory not in a state of submission ("Islam") to Allah, i.e., not ruled by Sharia law and not allied with Islamic states.

*dar al-Islam*—"House of Submission"; territory ruled by Sharia law.

*dar al-Sulh*—"House of Truce"; territory inhabited by Muslims but not governed by Sharia law, or non-Muslim territory allied with Islamic states.

*dhimma*—treaty of protection that may be granted to "People of the Book" (Jews and Christians) following their defeat by Muslim forces.

*dhimmi*—literally "protected"; non-Muslim, non-pagan (usually Jewish or Christian but also Zoroastrian) inhabitants of Islamic lands subjected to discriminatory laws and the *jizya* or poll tax.

*dhimmitude*—word coined by Bat Ye'or to describe the status of Jews, Christians, and Zoroastrians conquered but not killed or converted by Islamic jihad.

*hadith*—"report"; any of thousands of episodes from the life of Muhammad transmitted orally until written down in the eighth century AD; *sahih* (reliable or sound) hadiths are second only to the Koran in authority.

*Hijra*—"emigration"; Muhammad's flight from Mecca to Medina (Yathrib) in AD 622.

*Islam*—literally "submission" or "surrender."

*jihad*—literally "struggle" or "striving" in the way of Allah; in Islamic doctrine and history it is the violent struggle to bring the rule of Sharia law to new lands or to restore it to lands once previously ruled by Sharia.

*jizya*—poll or head tax prescribed by Sura 9:29 to be paid by Christian and Jews in Muslim-held territory.

*Kaba*—"cube"; the Meccan temple in which numerous pagan idols were housed before Muhammad's conquest of Mecca in AD 632, which is still the most venerated object in Islam; the Kaba's cornerstone is believed to be a stone that fell from heaven on which Abraham was to sacrifice his son, Ishmael (not Isaac).

*Koran*—"recitation"; the perfect, unalterable, verbatim words of Allah revealed to the Prophet Muhammad through the Archangel Gabriel.

*Mecca*—holiest city of Islam; place of Muhammad's birth in AD 570; its Great Mosque contains the Kaba stone; early period in Muhammad's life where more peaceful verses of the Koran were revealed; site of Muhammad's victory over the Quraish in AD 630.

*Medina*—"city," short for "city of the Prophet"; second holiest city of Islam; destination of Muhammad's *Hijra* (emigration) in AD 622; later period in Muhammad's life where more violent verses of the Koran were revealed; site of third major battle fought by Muhammad against the Quraish tribe from Mecca; formerly called Yathrib.

*Muhammad*—literally, "the praised one."

*razzia*—"raid"; acts of piracy on land or sea by Muslims against infidels.

*Sharia*—Islamic law; the codified commands and precedents from the Koran and the Sunnah.

*Sira*—"life"; abbreviation of *Sirat Rasul Allah*, or "Life of the Prophet of God"; the canonical biography of the Prophet Muhammad written in the eighth century by Ibn Ishaq and later edited by Ibn Hisham.

*Sunnah*—the "way" of the Prophet Muhammad; includes his teachings, traditions, and example.

*Sura*—a chapter of the Koran.

*taqiyya*—"dissimulation"; religious deception practiced by Muslims to deceive non-Muslims about their intentions and/or capabilities.

*Uhud*—second major battle fought by Muhammad against the Quraish tribe from Mecca.

*Umar*—second "rightly-guided" Caliph; ruled AD 634–44, succeeded Abu Bakr; conquered the Holy Land.

*Uthman*—third "rightly-guided" Caliph; ruled AD 644–56, succeeded Umar; compiled the Koran in book form.

*Yathrib*—city to which Muhammad made the *Hijra* (emigration) in AD 622; renamed Medina.

# BIBLIOGRAPHY

Adams, John and Thomas Jefferson in "Quotes from the Founding Fathers." *USDOJ and Government Watch*. http://www.dojgov.net/Liberty_Watch.htm.

Ahmed, Akbar S. *Islam Today: A Short Introduction to the Muslim World*. New York, NY: I. B. Tauris, 1999.

Al-Bana, Imam Shaheed Hasan. *Jihad*. United Kingdom: Prelude, 1997. http://www.youngmuslims.ca/online_library/books/jihad.

Balakian, Peter. *The Burning Tigris*. New York: HarperCollins, 2003.

Bat Ye'or. *Eurabia: The Euro-Arab Axis*. Madison: Fairleigh Dickinson University Press, 2005.

———. *Jihad and Dhimmitude: Where Civilizations Collide*. Madison: Fairleigh Dickinson University Press, 2001.

———. *The Decline of Eastern Christianity under Islam*. Madison: Fairleigh Dickinson University Press, 1996.

Belloc, Hilaire. *The Great Heresies*. Rockford: Tan Books and Publishers, 1991.

Bostom, Andrew, ed. *The Legacy of Jihad*. Amherst: Prometheus, 2005.

Braude, Joseph. "Moderate Muslims and Their Radical Leaders" in the New Republic, February 27, 2006. http://www.tnr.com/doc.mhtml?i=20060227&s=braude022706&c=2.

Emerson, Steven. *American Jihad*. Free Press, 2003.

Fergosi, Paul. *Jihad in the West: Muslim Conquests from the 7th to the 21st Centuries*. Amherst: Prometheus, 1998.

Fitzgerald, Hugh. "Islam for Infidels." http://www.jihadwatch.org/ archives/004628.php.

Hiskett, Mervyn. *Some to Mecca Turn to Pray*. St Alban's: Claridge Press, 1993.

Horowitz, David. *Unholy Alliance: Radical Islam and the American Left*. Regnery, 2004.

Ibn Ishaq. *The Life of Muhammad*. Alfred Guillaume, trans. Oxford: Oxford University Press, 2004.

Ibn Warraq. *What the Koran Really Says*. Amherst: Prometheus, 2002.

———. *Why I Am Not a Muslim*. Amherst: Prometheus, 1995.

Izetbegovic, Alija. *Islamic Declaration*. Sarajevo: Bosnia, 1990. http://www.srpska-mreza.com/library/facts/alija.html.

Johnstone, Diane. *Fools' Crusade.* Monthly Review Press, 2002.

Khan, Dr. Muhammad Muhsin, "Translation of Sahih Al-Bukhari." http://www.usc.edu/dept/MSA/fundamentals/hadithsunnah/bukhari.

Khan, Dr. Muhammad Muhsin and Dr. Muhammad Taqi-ud-Din Al Hilali, trans. *Interpretation of the Meanings of the Noble Quran.* (Riyadh: Dar-us-Salaam, 1996).

———. *Interpretation of the Meanings of the Noble Quran.* Riyadh: Dar-us-Salaam, 1996. http://dar-us-salam.com/TheNobleQuran.

Nasr, Seyyed Hossein. *Ideals and Realities in Islam.* Aquarian rev. ed. New York, NY: George Allen & Unwin, 2011. National Intelligence Council. *Mapping the Global Future.* http://www.cia.gov/nic/NIC_globaltrend2020.html.

Qutb, Sayyid. *Islam and Universal Peace.* American Trust Publications, 1977.

Pipes, Daniel. "Denying [Islamist] Terrorism" in the *New York Sun*, February 8, 2005. http://www.danielpipes.org/article/2396.

Ponte, Lowell. "Goodbye Europe" in *Frontpagemag.com*, March 28, 2006. http://www.frontpagemag.com/Articles/ReadArticle.asp? ID=21820.

Richards, Vernon. *Islam Undressed* (e-book), 2005. http://www. islamundressed.com.

Sell, Rev. Edward. *The Historical Development of the Qur'an.* (Facsimile of [probably] the 4th ed., London, 1923), People International, Tunbridge Wells, England, 1989. http://www.muham madanism.org/Canon_Sell/Quran/default.htm.

Spencer, Robert. *Islam Unveiled.* San Francisco: Encounter Books, 2002.

———. *The Myth of Islamic Tolerance.* Prometheus, 2005.

———. "Tarheel Jihad" in *Frontpagemag.com*, March 8, 2006. http://www.frontpagemag.com/Articles/ReadArticle.asp?ID=21554.

———. "Terror Denial" in *Frontpagemag.com*, March 6, 2005. http://www.frontpagemag.com/Articles/ReadArticle.asp?ID=17959.

Taheri, Amir. *Holy Terror.* Bethesda: Adler & Adler, 1987.

Tocqueville, Alexis de. "Letter to Arthur de Gobineau," October 22, 1843, in *Tocqueville Oeuvres Completes, vol. IX.* Paris: Gallimard, 1959.

Trifkovic, Serge. *The Sword of the Prophet.* Boston: Regina Orthodox Press, 2002.

———. *Defeating Jihad.* Boston: Regina Orthodox Press, 2006.

US State Department, Office of Counterterrorism, "Center for Defense Information Terrorism Project." April 2005. http://www. state.gov/s/ct/rls/fs/37191.htm.

Watt, William Montgomery. *Muhammad: Prophet and Statesman.* Oxford: Oxford University Press, 1961.

# INDEX